Campaign for Corinth
Blood in Mississippi

Civil War Campaigns and Commanders Series

Campaign for Corinth
Blood in Mississippi

Steven Nathaniel Dossman

Best Wishes —   5 - 21-06

Steven Nathaniel Dossman

McWhiney Foundation Press
McMurry University
Abilene, Texas

Library of Congress Cataloging-in-Publication Data

Dossman, Steven Nathaniel.
  Campaign for Corinth : blood in Mississippi /
by Steven Nathaniel Dossman.—1st ed.
    p. cm.—(Civil War campaigns and commanders series)
  Includes bibliographical references and index.
  ISBN-13: 978-1-893114-51-7 (pbk. : alk. paper)
  ISBN-10: 1-893114-51-1 (pbk. : alk. paper) 1. Corinth,
Battle of, Corinth, Miss., 1862. I. Title. II. Series.

    E474.44.D67 2006
    973.7'31—dc22

                                          2005032981

McWhiney Foundation Press
McMurry University, Box 637
Abilene, Texas 79697
(325) 793-4682
www.mcwhiney.org.

Printed in the United States of America

Distributed by Texas A&M University Press Consortium
1-800-826-8911
www.tamu.edu/upress

ISBN 978-1-893114-51-7
10 9 8 7 6 5 4 3 2 1

Book Designed by Rosenbohm Graphic Design

To my parents, with love and devotion,

To my professors, with gratitude and respect,

And to the soldiers of the blue and the gray,
with honor and tribute.

CONTENTS

CAMPAIGNS AND COMMANDERS SERIES

Map Key

Geography

	Trees
	Marsh
	Fields
	Strategic Elevations
	Rivers
	Tactical Elevations
)|(	Fords
	Orchards
— · — · —	Political Boundaries

Human Construction

⅀)(	Bridges
+++++++++	Railroads
	Tactical Towns
● ○	Strategic Towns
□ ■	Buildings
†	Church
✕	Roads

Military

▬ ▬	Union Infantry
▭ ▭	Confederate Infantry
▱ ◨	Cavalry
ιΙι	Artillery
⚑	Headquarters
△ △△ / △ △ / △ △△	Encampments
◇ ⊥	Fortifications
⊓⊓⊓⊓	Permanant Works
∼∼∼	Hasty Works
⊸⊸⊸⊸	Obstructions
☆ ✸ ✦ ✀	Engagements
⬭	Warships
◀▬	Gunboats
▬▬	Casemate Ironclad
▬◉▬	Monitor
↰ ⇒	Tactical Movements
⟶	Strategic Movements

Maps by
Donald S. Frazier, Ph.D.
Abilene, Texas

BIOGRAPHICAL SKETCHES

MAPS

PHOTOGRAPHS

Campaign for Corinth

1
"HELL OR CORINTH"

Many a vanish'd year and age,
And tempest's breath, and battle's rage,
Have Swept o'er Corinth; yet she stands
A fortress form'd to Freedom's hands.
—Lord Byron, *The Siege of Corinth*

Confederate Gen. Pierre Gustave Toutant Beauregard could see no other alternative. Mired in trenches, heavily outnumbered and outsupplied by the enemy, his army was wracked with hunger and disease. The cold arithmetic of war was clear in its calculations of defeat. Another battle would only serve to prove the futility of the situation, and put the army at risk as well—a loss the South could not afford. Regretfully, but resolutely, Beauregard gave the order to evacuate.

Corinth, Mississippi, was absolutely vital to the Confederate war effort, and its evacuation in May 1862 would resonate as one of the early turning points of the war. After a nearly two month long siege, the town fell to one of the largest military forces assembled in United States history up to that point, the enormous 120,000 man Union army under Maj. Gen. Henry Halleck. In the Western campaigns of 1862, few locations would share such importance and prominence as Corinth. The town was strategically valuable for one reason— it contained the intersection of the two most critical railroads in the South. Corinth was the site of the junction of the Memphis and Charleston line with the Mobile and Ohio, the crucial chains that linked the Confederacy together. The capture of Corinth would seriously hamper the South's ability to transport men and supplies from the Trans-Mississippi to the Eastern Theater, and would also provide the Federals with an excellent base to continue opening the Mississippi River Valley. The Union army could then proceed with the conquest of the major industrial centers of Chattanooga and Atlanta. The Mississippi Central Railroad, which ran north to south from Jackson, Tennessee, to Jackson, Mississippi, intersected with the Memphis and Charleston Railroad only fifty-two miles to the west of Corinth, and the Tennessee River with its floating avenue of supply was only some twenty miles away to the east. In a region that had few major roads, the loss of the railroads would be catastrophic to the infant Confederacy. To the policy architects of either side, the intersection of these tracks in Corinth constituted the most strategic three feet of dirt in the entire Western Theater.[1]

The city of Corinth was nothing more than a small hamlet of a mere 2,800 residents and 300 buildings. In many ways it was typical of most southern settlements, made up mainly of rural subsistence farmers, with a few large land and slave owners. It was not plantation country, and therefore the elected representatives of Tishomingo County voted for cooperation rather than separation at the state secession convention. To the citizens of Corinth, day-to-day survival was more important than either slavery or states' rights.[2]

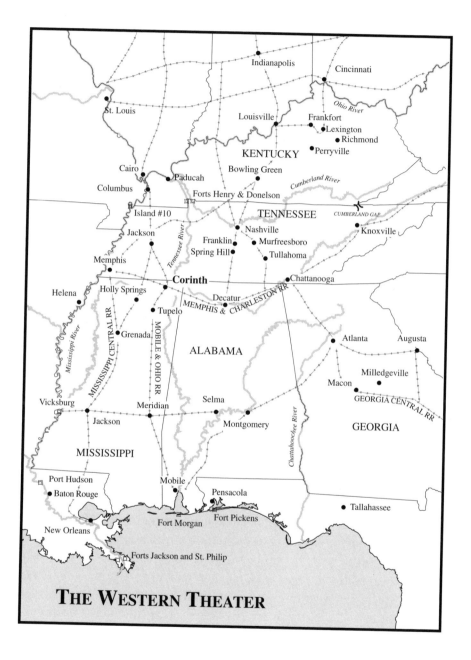

THE WESTERN THEATER

The land surrounding this southern citadel was as uninviting as the town. Northern Mississippi was a wild and barely settled country that produced men just as brutal as the landscape, such as the ferocious Confederate Gen. Nathan Bedford Forrest. One Missouri Rebel described it to be "the driest and dreariest of counties, barren, hilly and sandy, with crawfish soil where it was not covered with sand, and water of a milkish color, a sickly taste and demoralizing tendency." Scattered small streams and swamps dotted the country, producing mud and malaria, but little fluid fit for human consumption. The hot southern summer forced settlers to dig wells down as far as 100 to 300 feet to reach suitable water supplies. The limited amount of clean drinking water sustained the small population of the area, but was completely inadequate to provide for the hundreds of thousands of men and animals that would be campaigning there. Corinth was surrounded by low, rolling ridges and dense forests of red oak, white oak, and pine trees that limited visibility and troop movement, and created a natural shelter for irregular bands of partisan guerrillas.[3]

Confederate fortunes in the West had plummeted since the beginning of 1862. In September of the previous year, Gen. Albert Sidney Johnston had assumed command of the expansive Department Number 2, which stretched laterally over five hundred miles from Kentucky to Indian Territory, and included the northern parts of Louisiana, Mississippi, and Alabama. This vast amount of territory constituted the South's left flank, and to defend the area Johnston could only muster around 50,000 men, concentrated in isolated garrisons across the front. Facing Johnston were 90,000 Union troops poised to take the offensive against the ill-prepared Confederates. Unlike Virginia, where the rivers ran west to east and generally provided a natural barrier to invasion, in the West, rivers flowed north to south deep into the heartland of Dixie, a dangerous opening inviting a Federal thrust. The three largest and longest rivers were guarded by Fort Henry on the Tennessee, Fort Donelson on the Cumberland,

ULYSSES S. GRANT

Born in Point Pleasant, Ohio, in 1822, Grant's original name was Hiram Ulysses. When a congressman mistakenly put Ulysses Simpson (his mother's maiden name) on his application to the United States Military Academy, he gained a new name. Cadets called him Sam, and later he became famous as U.S. Grant. He graduated from West Point in 1843, twenty-first out of a class of thirty-nine. During the Mexican War, Grant had great admiration for Gen. Zachary Taylor, though he won battle distinction while serving under Winfield Scott. Ordered to the Pacific Coast after the war, he began to drink because of loneliness for his wife, resulting in his decision to resign his commission in July 1854. He was a failure as a civilian, and finally returned to his home town of Galena, Illinois, to work for the family business. When secession came, it was only with the aid of Congressmen Elihu B. Washburne that Grant gained a post in the army. Grant's career took off quickly, however. He gained national prominence with his "unconditional surrender" victory at Fort Donelson in February 1862. Though accused of allowing his forces to be surprised at Shiloh in April 1862, Grant's determined counter attack on the second day of the battle drove the Confederates back to Corinth. His masterful campaign for

Vicksburg in the spring and summer of 1863 marked him as one of the great military leaders of the conflict. Grant quickly gained overall command of the western theater of the war and relived the Confederate siege of Chattanooga in November 1863. Raised to the rank of lieutenant general in March 1864, Grant became commander of all Union armies and moved East to direct the Army of the Potomac's eventual victory over Robert E. Lee's Army of Northern Virginia. He was promoted to full general and held overall army command until 1869 when he became president of the United States for two terms. He later suffered repeated financial reverses and fought his last battle against his most fatal enemy, throat cancer, which claimed victory over him in 1885. Grant's memoirs, completed just before his death, were one of the most successful books ever published and left his family financially secure after his death. An unimpressive looking man, Grant had the ability to plot strategy that encompassed the continent and recognized the changing nature of war. He had a decisiveness that allowed him to react to battle field conditions calmly and surely. Where other generals might retreat, Grant continued pressing forward.

Henry W. Halleck

Born in Westernville, New York, in 1814, Halleck attended Union College where he made Phi Beta Kappa, and the United States Military Academy where he graduated third in his class of thirty-one in 1839. A member of the West Point faculty, Halleck later helped build fortifications in New York harbor, and traveled to France to study that nation's military organization and defense systems. In 1844, Halleck wrote *Report on the Means of National Defense*, and later gave a series of lectures that were published as the immensely influential *Elements of Military Art and Science*. Halleck then translated into English Antoine Henri Jomini's 4 volume *Vie Politique et Militaire de Napoleon*. Halleck and Sherman traveled to California together during the Mexican War, where he held a host of military government positions, including secretary of state. When California became a state, Halleck remained there as a military engineer but simultaneously held civilian positions including an attorney in San Francisco and a manager of a quicksilver mine. He resigned his army commission in 1854 to concentrate on his civilian legal and business activities which made him one of San Francisco's richest men. Halleck was a leader of the state's militia when secession came. He returned to the United States Army as a major general and,

and the mighty Mississippi River was protected by a bastion on the lower tip of Missouri named Island No. 10. Johnston bought time to strengthen his command by presenting a bold front, and threatening to take the offensive, which kept the Federals preoccupied for a precious few months.[4]

In January 1862, a small Rebel army was routed at the battle of Mill Springs, Kentucky, and in February Brig. Gen. Ulysses S. Grant captured Forts Henry and Donelson, cracking Johnston's thin defensive line. Grant became a national celebrity overnight, and soon the press had given new meaning to his initials, christening him "Unconditional Surrender" Grant. This was an unexpected display of talent from a man who until the fall of Fort Sumter had been less than successful

although Winfield Scott hoped he would be his replacement as commanding general, Halleck instead replaced John C. Fremont as head of the Department of Missouri. Halleck brought order to the region and received promotion to command of the Department of the Mississippi. He then oversaw Grant's victories at Forts Henry and Donelson and at Shiloh and then massed troops in the region to take Corinth in May 1862, although it took him a month to do so. In July 1862, Lincoln named Halleck commander of all Union armies, and the general moved to Washington. Halleck demonstrated the ability to administer the army, but did not take to the field to command any part of the army directly. In March 1864, when Lincoln named Grant the new commanding general, Halleck became the first chief of staff in American military history. In April 1865, with the war over, Halleck was sent to command the Department of Virginia and the Army of the James, and in August 1865 he became commander of the Military Division of the Pacific. In 1869, Halleck moved to Louisville, Kentucky, to take command of the Military Division of the South. He died there in 1872 and is buried in Brooklyn, New York. Nicknamed "Old Brains" by his soldiers after the capture of Corinth, Halleck was never an aggressive military leader. Sherman admired him until the conflict's last days, even when Halleck accused Sherman of collaborating with the enemy in his peace terms with Joseph E. Johnston. Most other Union officials came to have a low opinion of him earlier than Sherman, and Lincoln called Halleck "little more than a first rate clerk." Halleck was an excellent administrator but, because of physical and psychological factors, had difficulty rising above mundane matters to provide the inspiring leadership the times required.

in life. After achieving both a West Point education and an impressive record in the Mexican War, Grant had let the loneliness of frontier duty and alcohol get the better of him, and he had resigned his commission to return to his family. A series of financial schemes went bust, which forced a cash-strapped Grant to work as a clerk in his father's store. When the war broke out, his previous experience and political connections earned him a general's commission of volunteers.[5]

Grant's fellow West Point cadet, Confederate Gen. Richard Ewell, was one of the few men on either side who initially recognized Grant's potential for leadership, stating that "There is one West Pointer, I think in Missouri, little known, and whom I hope the Northern people will not find out. I mean Sam Grant. . . . I should fear him more than any of their officers I have yet heard of. He is not a man of genius, but he is clear-headed, quick and daring." After fighting a sharp engagement at Belmont, Missouri, Grant found himself under the command of Halleck, who, unlike Ewell, had little respect for the poorly-regarded Grant. Now, given a chance to prove himself, Grant had stunned both his enemies and his superiors. Forts Henry and Donelson were the first decisive victories of the war for the North, yielding more than 12,000 prisoners and a substantial amount of military supplies.[6]

With the Tennessee and Cumberland Rivers opened to Federal navigation, the North used these waterways as a thoroughfare to the southern heartland, penetrating deeply with its superior naval power. From there on it had been a long successful march southward, forcing the Confederates completely out of Kentucky, taking Nashville–the first southern state capital to fall–and much of central Tennessee, including the invaluable Cumberland Iron Works at Clarksville, surpassed only by Richmond's Tredegar Iron Works in production. Grant's victories had earned him a promotion to major general, but had also attracted the jealousy of his commanding officer, General Halleck.[7]

After Fort Donelson fell, Halleck even went so far as to demand recognition and rewards for the success from then General-in-Chief McClellan. "Make Buell, Grant, and Pope major generals of volunteers and give me command of the West. I ask this in return for Forts Henry and Donelson," Halleck wrote to McClellan. To his dismay, only Grant received the promotion, and Halleck was forced to be content with commanding the Department of Missouri. Later, in March, when Halleck lost contact with Grant's army due to a telegraph communications breakdown, and Halleck heard rumors that Grant was drinking again, he attempted to have him relieved of command, only to rescind the order when the charges proved unsubstantiated. Grant's status improved somewhat when

Halleck was finally promoted to oversee the West, leaving Grant to remain with the Army of the Tennessee. However, there was a growing degree of mistrust towards Grant in headquarters, where his old drinking habits haunted the mind of Henry Halleck.[8]

In response to the crisis created by the loss of the forts, Confederate Gen. Albert Sidney Johnston began using the network of rails and roads to concentrate troops from all over the West in Corinth, to form what he designated as the Army of the Mississippi. Soon Johnston had gathered an army of 40,335 men, nearly equal to Grant's 42,682–man Army of the Tennessee. In a gamble even more daring than his previous bluff of strength in Kentucky, Johnston conceived of an attack to save the railroad and regain the lost territory before Grant could be reinforced. Johnston's men had little training or experience, but they possessed the raw recruit's sense of optimism and a hunger to strike at the hated Northerners.[9]

In early April 1862, Johnston led the Army of the Mississippi out of Corinth in hopes of destroying Grant's invading force, camped only twenty-two miles to the north at Pittsburgh Landing. On the morning of the April 6, Confederate forces caught the Union army completely unprepared near a small Methodist Church named Shiloh. Only Grant's stable leadership and the timely arrival of Union Gen. Don Carlos Buell's Army of the Ohio that night saved the Federals from complete destruction. The shocking bloodshed of the battle of Shiloh, which claimed 23,741 casualties and mortally wounded Johnston as well, failed to halt the advancing soldiers in blue. Unchanged in his opinion of Grant and now blaming him for the near disaster, Halleck arrived to assume personal command. Three separate Union armies–the Army of the Tennessee, the Army of the Ohio, and the Federal Army of the Mississippi–were combined into one vast horde under Halleck, who proceeded to advance cautiously to Corinth.[10]

Grant's recently gained skillful reputation suffered under the intense scrutiny of Shiloh. One of his own men wrote in his diary that, "Genl Grant is hated and *despised* by all the men and cursed ever since the 6th of April." The fickle press was even more vehement in its criticism, labeling him "Ulysses *Surprise* Grant," and powerful men in Washington began calling for his removal from command. The reports and accusations of incompetence did little to upset the solid nerves of Grant, who wrote to Congressman Elihu Washburne saying that, "notoriety has no charms for me and could I render the same services that I hope it has been my fortune to render our just cause, without being known in the matter, it would be infinately prefferable [*sic*] to me." The cries of the editors and politicians for Grant to be replaced soon reached all the way to the White House, where President Lincoln stated bluntly, "I can't spare this man. He fights."[11]

What did upset Grant was his new assignment from Halleck, as second-in-command of the army. The appointment gave Grant little responsibility and effectively promoted him out of the way. Years later, in his memoirs, Grant would describe his miserable situation as, "for myself I was little more than an observer. Orders were sent direct to the right wing or reserve, ignoring me, and advances were made from one line of intrenchments to another without notifying me. My position was so embarrassing in fact that I made several applications during the siege to be relieved."[12]

After Shiloh, the Confederates withdrew to Corinth, where the two exhausted armies received reinforcements and settled down for siege. Gen. P.G.T. Beauregard replaced the fallen Johnston, and while he was attempting to rebuild his shattered army, news arrived that Island No. 10 had surrendered on April 8, costing the South another 7,000 men as prisoners of war. This Union victory opened the Mississippi to Fort Pillow, which protected Memphis. Despite these victories, Halleck was so fearful of a surprise attack that it took almost a month for him to advance his huge army the twenty-two miles to Corinth, progressing less than a mile a day and entrenching every night.[13]

Beauregard had little time for concern, however, for the situation in Corinth was deteriorating rapidly. Thousands of wounded men overwhelmed the surgeons and medical facilities, turning every available building into a makeshift hospital. The overcrowding of the army strained the insufficient water supply, which was already lower than normal due to an unusually dry spring. Sanitation was unknown, and soon dysentery, typhoid, and measles were raging furiously. Private Sam Watkins described his suffering, stating that "we became starved skeletons; naked and ragged rebels." Beauregard himself was ill, as were more than 18,000 of his men, while almost 5,000 were on detached duty, rendering his supposed 75,402 men to 52,706 weakened soldiers facing double their numbers.[14]

Living conditions in the Confederate ranks became nearly unbearable. One Texan in Corinth, S.B. Barron of the Third Texas Cavalry, recalled that "the water we had to drink was bad, very bad, and the rations none of the best." More wells were dug throughout the area, which provided a temporary supply of a "mean, milky-looking fluid," but as the heat and demand increased, the wells were sunk to ever increasing depths. Barron noted that his "horse would not drink a drop of the water the men had to use, and if I failed to ride him to a small running branch some two miles away he would go without drinking. The rations consisted mainly of flour, made into poor camp biscuit, and the most unpalatable pickled beef." Confederate Col. Lawrence Sullivan ("Sul") Ross grumbled that Corinth was "a Malarious sickly spot, fitten only for alligators & snakes."[15]

The food was so wretched that Barron wrote that "I could no more eat one of our biscuits than I could have eaten a stone, and as for the beef, I could as easily swallowed a piece

of skunk. The mere sight of it was nauseating." Barron further complained that "had I not been at headquarters doubtless I would have starved to death, since there we were able to get a ham or something else extra occasionally, and I managed to eat, but barely enough to keep soul and body together." The supply crisis only worsened as the siege continued and southern logistics crumbled.[16]

The area surrounding Corinth was littered with the remains of the Confederate retreat from Shiloh, such as discarded baggage, equipment, and bodies. A soldier from Iowa, Sgt. Cyrus Boyd, remarked that it was "the most Godforsaken country I

The 31st Ohio Infantry constructing earthworks during the siege of Corinth, May 1862. *Library of Congress.*

ever saw" and "one vast *graveyard."* The spring rains had washed the earth from the recent shallow graves of men and horses, and the decomposing remains were a ghastly sight even for the veterans. The Iowan further described the horror, saying that *"Skulls* and *toes* are sticking from beneath the clay all around and the heavy wagons *crush* the bodies turning up the bones of the burried, making this one vast Golgotha." Some unlucky men had the misfortune of camping in these makeshift cemeteries, where neither the living nor the dead rested in peace.[17]

Corinth was defended by miles of earthworks, built upon the ridges around town. Beauregard wired Richmond of the seriousness of the Federal threat, warning that "If defeated here we can lose the Mississippi Valley and probably our cause, whereas we could even afford to lose for a while Charleston and Savannah for the purpose of defeating Buell's army, which would not only insure us the valley of Mississippi, but our independence." Halleck agreed, stating that,

EARL VAN DORN

Born in Mississippi in 1820, Van Dorn graduated from the U.S. Military Academy in 1842, fifty-second in his class of fifty-six. As a brevet second lieutenant, he was posted to the 7th Infantry. He owned an exceptionally active career, serving in various garrison and frontier commands. Twice brevetted for the Mexican War, he was promoted to first lieutenant in 1847 and served against the Seminoles in Florida. In 1855, Van Dorn became a captain in the newly organized 2d U.S. Cavalry, an elite regiment that included Albert Sidney Johnston, Robert E. Lee, George H. Thomas, William J. Hardee, and John B. Hood. In Texas, he fought numerous actions against the Comanches and was wounded in an engagement in Indian Territory. With Mississippi's withdrawal from the Union in 1860, Van Dorn, having been promoted to major, tendered his resignation to serve his native state. He became a brigadier general of Mississippi state troops and rose to major general commanding state troops upon Jefferson Davis's election as president of the Confederate States. Van Dorn entered Confederate service in March 1861, and was commissioned a colonel. He briefly commanded Forts Jackson and St. Philip that guarded the southern

"Richmond and Corinth are now the great strategic points of the war, and our success at these points should be insured at all hazards."[18]

Into this drastic situation came a dashing, debonair Confederate major general named Earl Van Dorn, part of the reinforcements that were rushed to Beauregard's aid. A friend once described Van Dorn as "the most remarkable man the State of Mississippi ever produced." He was a romantic cavalier, impetuous and courageous, ready to gamble everything for glory and honor. Another West Point alumnus in a war of many, he had made his name fighting in Mexico and against Indians on the Texas frontier. He graduated fifty-second out of fifty-six in the West Point class of 1842 that included future

approaches to New Orleans, but was soon appointed commander of the Department of Texas, where his performance earned him promotion to brigadier general in June 1861. Ordered to Virginia soon afterwards, he was elevated to major general and commanded a division under Gen. Joseph E. Johnston. Van Dorn returned to the West in January 1862, where he commanded the Trans-Mississippi District of Department Number Two and the small Army of the West. In March, his forces were defeated at the Battle of Pea Ridge. Van Dorn then led his army across the Mississippi River to reinforce Gen. P.G.T. Beauregard's beleaguered force at Corinth, Mississippi. Given command of the Department of Southern Mississippi and East Louisiana, he worked to defend Vicksburg, but his harsh administration of the department led to his removal in July 1862. After being soundly defeated at Corinth in October, Van Dorn assumed command of the cavalry under his successor in Mississippi, Gen. John C. Pemberton. Much better suited for a cavalry command, Van Dorn turned in his finest Civil War performance with his December 1862 raid on Gen. U.S. Grant's Holly Springs depot. In addition to destroying tons of Federal supplies, the raid delayed Grant's advance on Vicksburg. Van Dorn then headed a cavalry division in Gen. Braxton Bragg's Army of Tennessee and was successful in several clashes in central Tennessee. A handsome and dashing figure, Van Dorn, although married, was a known ladies' man, whose transgressions often drew the consternation of fellow officers and citizens alike. While headquartered at Spring Hill, Tennessee, he spent much time with the young wife of a local physician, and in May 1863 the aggrieved husband, Dr. James Peters, confronted Van Dorn in the general's quarters and shot him to death.

Confederate Gen. James Longstreet, and future Union generals Don Carlos Buell, John Pope, and William S. Rosecrans. Ulysses S. Grant happened to be in the class below him. Van Dorn's friends at the academy nicknamed the 5 foot 6 inch cadet "Buck," and it stayed with him throughout his career. Before secession Van Dorn served as a major in Albert Sidney Johnston's vaunted 2nd U.S. Cavalry Regiment, which included future Civil War generals Robert E. Lee, William J. Hardee, and George Thomas in its ranks. While leading an expedition against the Comanches in Texas Van Dorn was severely wounded by arrows, one striking his left arm just above the wrist and a second entering on his right side, cutting through the ribs, stomach, and left lung before it exited. Amazingly, he not only survived, but managed to kill one of the warriors who shot him before he collapsed.[19]

Further evidence of Van Dorn's reckless passion for life was his unabashed procurement of a concubine while stationed in Texas, by which he fathered three children, while still maintaining a wife and family back home in Mississippi. He did not provide or care for these illegitimate offspring, although they did carry his name. Van Dorn managed to keep his affairs from his wife, but adultery would be a perennial bad habit for the rest of his life. Van Dorn was a handsome ladies' man, but he was equally as willing to fight as he was to romance. At the outbreak of the Civil War Van Dorn played a major role in the surrender of Federal troops in Texas and in the capture of the steamer *Star of the West*, which had previously been the target of the first hostile shots of the war in a failed relief expedition to Fort Sumpter in January 1861. For his efforts Van Dorn received national fame and notoriety, including a five thousand dollar bounty from a Yankee newspaper, which he considered a badge of pride.[20]

Van Dorn's first major assignment was commanding the savage and overlooked Trans-Mississippi Department. Almost instantly upon his arrival in February 1862, he mounted a risky offensive to force the Federals out of Arkansas and begin an anticipated conquest of Missouri. With an odd ragtag assortment of 16,000 men, which included Texas frontiersmen, boys from the Arkansas hills, and a few Native Americans, he rashly attacked the Union force at Pea Ridge in early March. The weather, terrain, and 10,500 Federal troops proved to be too much, and his remarkably diverse army nearly disintegrated in a harrowing retreat through the cold snows of the Ozarks. Van Dorn, always so popular with the ladies, was abandoned by Lady Luck. Undaunted by his failure though determined to restore his reputation, in early April Van Dorn transported what was left of his self-styled "Army of the West" across the Mississippi to reinforce Beauregard at Corinth. Upon his arrival a nurse wrote in her journal, "Corinth is more

STERLING PRICE

Born in Virginia in 1809, Price attended Hampden-Sydney College and studied law. He moved with his family to Missouri in 1830 where he served in the state legislature and in 1844 was elected to the U.S. House of Representatives. Price resigned from Congress to lead a regiment of Missouri troops in the Mexican War, and was promoted to brigadier general of volunteers in 1848. Price was governor of Missouri from 1853 to 1857, and president of the Missouri convention that voted against secession, but a dispute with radicals prompted his break from the Unionist ranks. He offered his services to secessionist Gov. C.F. Jackson and accepted command of the Missouri state militia. Price worked to maintain peace in Missouri, but after negotiations with Union leaders broke down in June 1861, he prepared his troops to oppose Federal forces. Price's men combined with Gen. Ben McCulloch's Confederate troops to defeat the Federals at Wilson's Creek, Missouri, in August 1861. Price captured Lexington, Missouri, in September before retreating into Arkansas where he led Missouri troops in Gen. Earl Van Dorn's Confederate force at Elkhorn Tavern, Arkansas, in March 1862. Following that defeat, the Missouri troops were mustered into Confederate service and Price was commissioned major general. Price was transferred to Mississippi, despite his fervent protest, where he suffered defeats at Iuka and  Corinth before returning to Arkansas. He was defeated again at Helena in 1863. Price supported Gen. E. Kirby Smith in repulsing Gen. Frederick Steele's Arkansas portion of the Red River Campaign in the spring of 1864. That fall, Price led an ambitious cavalry raid into Missouri, but after initial success, was turned back in eastern Kansas. After retreating through Indian Territory and northern Texas, Price's remnant returned to Arkansas in December. At the close of the war Price refused to surrender and escaped to Mexico. Upon the collapse of Maximilian's empire in 1866, Price returned to Missouri, where he died the following year. Called "Old Pap" by his men, Price was a devoted soldier. While his 1864 raid and subsequent exodus to Mexico have been highly romanticized, his overall military performance was largely unimpressive.

unhealthy than ever. The cars have just come in, loaded outside and inside with troops. They are Price's and Van Dorn's men, and are from Texas, Arkansas, Louisiana, and Missouri.

Poor fellows! they look as if they had seen plenty of hard service, which is true." Upon seeing Van Dorn's arrival a Confederate soldier noted that his commander appeared to be "more of a dandy than the general of an army. He was small, curley or kinkey headed, exquisitely dressed, was riding a beautiful bay horse, evidently groomed with as much care as his rider, who was small looking and frenchy."[21]

Van Dorn's second in command was the Missouri politician Maj. Gen. Sterling Price. The fifty-two-year-old had a grandfatherly appearance, and was called "Old Pap" by his beloved Missourians. He had served in both the state house and Governor's Mansion of his state, and had led a volunteer regiment in the Mexican War. Unlike many of his fellow officers, he was not a West Pointer, but owed his commission to his political prestige. Price had led his men throughout the early bitter campaigns in Missouri and Arkansas, fighting at Wilson's Creek, Lexington, and Pea Ridge. One female observer described him as "one of the finest looking men on horseback that I have ever seen. I have a picture of Lord Raglan in the same position, and I think that he and General Price are the image of each other." The months of service had endeared Price to his men, who blamed Van Dorn entirely for the Pea Ridge fiasco. After touring the impressive fortifications surrounding Corinth with Beauregard, Price referred to his capture of Lexington stating, "Well, these things may be fine; I never saw anything of the kind but once, and then I took them." Proud and defiant, Price crossed the Mississippi not by desire but by order. To Price, the thought of serving elsewhere while his home in Missouri was under northern occupation was almost treason.[22]

The sight of Corinth and its well-dressed officers impressed the rough looking but veteran Rebels of Van Dorn's command. One of those soldiers remembered that "the town was literally alive with officers and soldiers. There were more headquarters, more sentinels, and more red tape here than I had ever dreamed

A *Harper's Weekly* illustration of Maj. Gen. John Pope's advance into Corinth on May 30, 1862, from the June 21, 1862 issue.

of." The homespun, backwoods nature of the Trans-Mississippi Department was revealed when the soldier later stated that he had "not seen uniformed officers or men west of the Mississippi River, and had known nothing of red tape in the army."[23]

By late April, the North had captured New Orleans, depriving the South of its largest city and most vital port. Soon after that, Baton Rouge fell, and then Natchez, which further eroded Confederate control on the Mississippi River. Halleck maintained his stranglehold on Corinth into May, but the soldiers of both armies were suffering from exertion under the hot southern sun. A correspondent from the *Richmond Dispatch* complained of the well water that "with every pint of fluid one has to drink a half ounce of dirt. You feel it scrape the throat as it goes down, and after it gets to the stomach it lays as heavy and indigestible as a bed of mortar."[24]

Across the lines, Union troops were suffering as well. Federal Sgt. Cyrus Boyd wrote in his diary that "all the men look bad," and that "all of them have the diarrhea and are scarcely able to take care of themselves." He further lamented that the "*dead march* can be heard at all times from sun up until sun down in the camps around us—as they take one, two or three poor fellows and lay them in this cold and dismal wilderness in graves to be forever unknown." Surprisingly, in the heavily forested terrain of northern Mississippi, cut lumber was scarce and many men were laid to rest without a coffin. Boyd speculated that "if we remain here until July but few will be *alive.*" Some of those dead Union soldiers had written "Hell or Corinth" on their hatbands, displaying their desperation to capture the railhead.[25]

Beauregard had twice attempted a counterstroke against the Federals, but no serious fighting had occurred. Eventually the Confederate general felt the noose tightening, and on May 25 Beauregard decided that he had no choice other than to evacuate as soon as possible, and escape with what supplies and men he had left. The extensive preparations were made to the last detail, while the men in the ranks were told to be ready to mount an imminent attack. Captured prisoners and deserters reported these rumors to Halleck, who believed Beauregard's deception and immediately warned his commanders to be on alert. On the night May 29, the retreat began, with wooden "Quaker guns" replacing the outgoing cannon, and extra campfires lighting up the darkness. The Confederates made as much commotion as possible to sell the ruse, and even ran an empty train in and out of Corinth; complete with whistles, bands, and cheers to make it appear large numbers of reinforcements had arrived. The ruse was so successful that at 1:20 in the morning, Maj. Gen. John Pope wired Halleck that "the enemy is re-enforcing heavily, by trains, in my front and on my left. The cars are running constantly, and the cheering is immense every time they unload in front of me. I have no doubt, from all appearances, that I shall be attacked in heavy force at daylight."[26]

Daylight came, but the expected attack never materialized. The Federals advanced and were stunned to find Corinth empty, occupied only by the smoke from burning military stores. A member of the 7th Illinois Infantry wrote that "we are now camped near the rebel commissary; it is one vast heap of ruins; sugar and flour scattered all over the ground, molasses running in streams down the railroad. Everywhere the fields are strewn with tents, cooking utensils, army wagons, old trunks, rebel uniforms, flint lock muskets, &c., &c. It is indeed an apt illustration of the assumed confederacy."[27]

There was certainly little regret over the evacuation in the Confederate ranks. Tennessean Sam Watkins remembered bleakly that "we bade farewell to Corinth. Its history was black and dark and damning. No little speck of green oasis ever enlivened the dark recesses of our memory while at this place. It's a desert that lives only in bitter memories." Away from the sickness and privation of Corinth, the army's health and morale slowly revived, and the withdrawal was celebrated as a brilliant success.[28]

As the gray columns marched southward, General Price rode down the procession, receiving cheer after cheer from his men. Soon afterwards General Van Dorn followed, greeted only by a deafening roar of silence. One company of the 2nd Missouri felt pity for their commander's "hard treatment" and raised their rifles to present arms in an impromptu salute, to which Van Dorn responded by removing his cap. One witness later remarked that the tribute was "the first and only one I ever saw him receive from his soldiers." Although he held both a higher grade than Price as well as the confidence of Richmond, Van Dorn was painfully aware of whom the enlisted men of the Army of the West preferred to be their commander. Earl Van Dorn commanded the army, but Sterling Price commanded the loyalty and respect of the ranks.[29]

The Confederates retreated to Tupelo, Mississippi, following the Mobile and Ohio Railroad southward. It was a difficult march, made more so by the ever present lack of water. One Confederate officer recalled a humorous episode from the retreat, where he enabled some of his men to wet their throats. A "lank, lantern-jawed Mississippian," had been selling water to the thirsty soldiers for twenty five cents per canteen full, and was profiting handsomely. This enterprise continued until one stubborn Rebel refused to pay, and the local entrepreneur responded by removing the handle of the chain-pump in his well. The officer soon located a spring, and the men "tore away the pump, took the rope that corded his best bed and thus obtained a full supply of the coveted fluid." He remarked that it "was about the only invasion of private rights I witnessed during the war."[30]

A much more somber scene of the siege and evacuation was witnessed by a Confederate soldier who explained that "on the day we left Corinth I passed Booneville, a station ten miles below Corinth, and here were perhaps fifty sick men lying in the shade of the trees and bushes. One of the attendants with whom I was acquainted told me he had just returned from a tramp of two or three miles, after water for a wounded man. At every house he came to the well buckets had been taken off and hid, and he finally had to fill his canteen with brackish pond water." The writer further commented that "the mere recollection of those scenes causes a shudder to this day."[31]

Halleck left the Confederates to escape unmolested, wiring his commanders that "the main object now is to get the enemy far enough south to relieve our railroads from danger of an immediate attack. There is no object in bringing on a battle if this object can be obtained without one. I think by showing a bold front for a day or two the enemy will continue his retreat, which is all I desire." Halleck's decision infuriated many of his officers, including Grant, who knew that the fleeing Southerners would return to fight another day. Grant later wrote that "the victory was barren" and that a strong pursuit would have enabled "a bloodless advance to Atlanta, to Vicksburg, or to any other desired point south of Corinth in the interior of Mississippi." A Federal captain complained in his diary that "General Halleck did not seem to know anything more of what was going on in Corinth than I did. . . . We gained a victory at Corinth, that's all, and Halleck's over-caution prevented it from being much of one." Instead, in part due to President Lincoln's persuasion, Halleck divided his massive army into garrisons and began concentrating his attention on taking Chattanooga. Halleck had fumbled his greatest opportunity of the war, and the Confederate army he had allowed to escape would soon return seeking vengeance.[32]

For Grant, the culmination of the campaign was of little solace, as he still lay dormant in his duties under Halleck. He later recollected that "my position at Corinth, with a nominal command and yet no command, became so unbearable that I asked permission of Halleck to remove my headquarters to Memphis. I had repeatedly asked, between the fall of Donelson and the evacuation of Corinth, to be relieved from duty under Halleck; but all my applications were refused until the occupation of the town." Once the siege was over, Grant's request for leave was approved. As he prepared to depart, his old friend Maj. Gen. William T. Sherman visited and asked why he was going away. Grant replied, "Sherman, you know. You know that I am in the way here. I have stood it as long as I can, and can endure it no longer." Sherman advised Grant that his situation was certain to improve with time and persuaded him to remain with the army. Grant stayed, resolving to wait for a chance to be in the fighting once more.[33]

As Grant pondered his uncertain future, some fifty-two miles to the south, Earl Van Dorn waited impatiently for a second chance to purge the memory of Pea Ridge from the minds of his critics and men. Before the year 1862 ended, the reckless caviler would take that chance and challenge the reliable Grant. The ensuing battle would witness some of the most brutal carnage ever encountered in the war and ultimately decide the fate of the western Confederacy.

2

"The most anxious period of the war"

In late May 1862, another member of the West Point class of 1842 arrived in Corinth, one who would play a leading role in the impending campaign. Brig. Gen. William S. Rosecrans was an Ohioan who had graduated fifth in the class, a substantially higher rank than either his roommate Confederate Gen. James Longstreet, his classmate Earl Van Dorn, or his new superior Ulysses S. Grant, who graduated the following year. Rosecrans's high standing secured him an assignment to the exclusive Corps of Engineers, where he demonstrated such talent that he was made an instructor of engineering at the Academy. He saw no action during the Mexican War and resigned from the Army in 1853 to become a businessman manufacturing coal oil in Cincinnati. His life and promising entrepreneurial career were almost ended when a safety lamp exploded near his head, terribly burning him. After almost two years of convalescence he recovered, but permanent scars on his face would serve as a constant reminder of his close encounter with death.[1]

When the war erupted Rosecrans quickly volunteered as a staff officer for Maj. Gen. George McClellan, who soon gave him a field command in what would later become West Virginia. At the Battle of Rich Mountain, Rosecrans devised and led a flanking assault that completely routed the Confederates. McClellan, however, failed to attack frontally in support of Rosecrans's success, allowing the small southern force to escape. Nevertheless, Rosecrans won praise for his triumph, which was vital to establishing Federal control of the strategic Kanawha Valley. McClellan, however, won command of the Army of the Potomac thanks to his personal appropriation of his subordinate's victories, which instilled in Rosecrans a lasting mistrust of superiors.[2]

After McClellan, whom Rosecrans had designated as "that damned little cuss," was promoted to Washington, Rosecrans replaced him as commander of the Department of the Ohio, where Rosecrans bested Robert E. Lee's determined efforts to reclaim West Virginia in the fall of 1861. Union Maj. Gen. Henry Halleck, commanding the Federal Army of the Mississippi, welcomed Rosecrans' transfer to the West and gave him command of two divisions. Rosecrans was a quick tempered but capable commander, who would fight anyone who opposed him, regardless of the uniform they wore. He was dedicated both to the Catholic Church and cursing, a unique combination that earned him the admiration and respect of his men, who spoke of their general as "Old Rosy."[3]

While Rosecrans was traveling to his new assignment, Confederate fortunes in Mississippi were drying up as quickly as the water supply. Soon after the loss of Corinth, Gen. P.T.G. Beauregard ordered Fort Pillow to be abandoned as well, which left the key transportation and supply center of Memphis virtually unprotected. After a brief naval melee on

WILLIAM STARKE ROSECRANS

Born in Ohio in 1819, Rosecrans graduated from the U.S. Military Academy fifth in the class of 1842. Brevetted 2d lieutenant of engineers in 1842 and promoted to 2d lieutenant in 1843, he did not participate in the war with Mexico. Rosecrans became a 1st lieutenant in 1853, before resigning from the army in 1854. He was head of a Cincinnati kerosene refinery in 1861, but resigned to become an aide to Gen. George B. McClellan with the rank of colonel of engineers. In May he simultaneously became colonel of the 23rd Ohio Infantry and a brigadier general U.S. Army. During McClellan's operations in western Virginia, he commanded a brigade at Rich Mountain, and after McClellan left to assume command of the Union army, Rosecrans drove Robert E. Lee's Confederates from the area and made possible the erection of the state of West Virginia. In 1862, Rosecrans commanded the left wing of John Pope's Army of the Mississippi in the advance on Corinth following the Battle of Shiloh. He succeeded to command after Pope's transfer to Virginia. Rosecrans, now under General Grant's direction, fought in the bloody battles at Iuka and Corinth.

the river, the city fell on June 6 to the relentless Federal gunboats under Flag Officer Charles H. Davis. Only Vicksburg remained to hold the fractured Confederacy together on the Mississippi River. In a span of less than five months the South had lost enormous amounts of territory in the West, including the important industrial cities of Nashville, Clarksville, and Memphis, the vital port of New Orleans, the rail hub at Corinth, along with thousands of men either killed, wounded, sick, or captured, including their most promising commander, Gen. Albert Sidney Johnston. Now they lost Beauregard as well, who went on extended sick leave from the army in June, during the apex of the whole dismal affair.[4]

The northern juggernaut appeared unstoppable. After occupying Corinth, Halleck sent an expedition of 30,000 men

Rosecrans was appointed major general of volunteers in 1862, and went to Kentucky to replace Don Carlos Buell as commander of the Army of the Cumberland. At year's end he repulsed Braxton Bragg's Army of Tennessee at Murfreesboro with heavy losses on both sides. Honored in 1863 by Congress "for gallantry and good conduct at the Battle of Murfreesboro," Rosecrans, after a six month lull in operations, began a brilliant maneuver known as the Tullahoma Campaign that forced the Confederates from central Tennessee into the fortified railroad center of Chattanooga and then south into Georgia. At Chickamauga, where in September Bragg attacked and drove the Federals back into Chattanooga, Rosecrans suffered a crushing defeat that virtually ended his military career. He was superseded by Grant in October. Rosecrans commanded the Department of Missouri in 1864, and was promoted to brevet major general in 1865 "for gallant and distinguished service at the Battle of Stones River." He was honorably mustered out of volunteer service in 1866, and he resigned from the Regular Army in 1867. He was appointed by President Johnson as minister to Mexico, a post from which Grant, upon becoming president, removed him. During his remaining years, Rosecrans resided on his California ranch frequently complaining of "oil seepage into his water wells." He was elected to Congress in 1880, and served until 1885, rising to chairman of the Committee on Military Affairs. From 1885 to 1893 he was register of the Treasury. He also managed to have himself appointed brigadier general in the Regular Army in February and then retired in March 1889. He died in 1898, and was first buried in Los Angeles before being reinterred in 1902 in Arlington National Cemetery.

under Maj. Gen. Don Carlos Buell to gain control of East Tennessee, while his remaining men garrisoned the newly liberated areas and rebuilt the railroads. In the Eastern Theater, George McClellan's massive Union Army of the Potomac was slowly creeping up the peninsula toward Richmond, drawing closer every day. At no point since the beginning of the war had the South's prospects sunk so low, and it seemed to many observers that the Confederacy's complete collapse was assured before the year was out.[5]

It would take an aggressive and brilliant strategy to reverse this tide of defeat, from a perpetually declining pool of talented and tested generals. When the principal commander in the East, Gen. Joseph E. Johnston, was wounded at the battle of Seven Pines in late May, so soon after the death

BRAXTON BRAGG

Born in North Carolina in 1817, Bragg graduated from the U.S. Military Academy fifth in the 1837 class of fifty. He was first appointed 2d lieutenant 3rd Artillery, then promoted to 1st lieutenant in 1838, and on to captain in 1846. He participated in the Seminole War and won three brevet promotions for gallant conduct during the Mexican War. In 1849, Bragg married Eliza Brooks Ellis, daughter of a Louisiana sugar cane planter. After routine garrison duty on the frontier, he resigned his brevet lieutenant colonelcy in 1856 to become a Louisiana sugar planter. In 1861, Bragg was appointed a Confederate brigadier general and assigned to Pensacola, Florida, where he changed the volunteers he found there into drilled and disciplined soldiers. He was promoted to major general and assigned command of the Gulf Coast from Pensacola to Mobile. In 1862, he received orders to move his troops by rail to join Gen. A.S. Johnston's army at Corinth, Mississippi, for the Battle of Shiloh, during which Bragg served as army chief of staff and commanded a corps. After Johnston's death, upon the recommendation of his successor, Gen. P.G.T. Beauregard, Bragg was promoted to full general. In June, he in turn replaced General Beauregard when that officer took an unauthorized sick leave. Deciding to invade Kentucky, Bragg moved the bulk of his army from Tupelo,

of Albert Sidney Johnston at Shiloh, many feared the South could not overcome the acute loss of leadership. In the Confederate capital, President Jefferson Davis turned to the highly regarded, but relatively unproven Gen. Robert E. Lee for Richmond's salvation. In the West, Davis gave command to the more battle-tested Gen. Braxton Bragg, who faced a challenge just as daunting as his Virginia counterpart's. Both reorganized their armies and planed counteroffensives to regain lost territory and restore morale. Unless there was a drastic and sudden alteration of the strategic situation, all dreams of an independent southern nation would be destroyed.[6]

Mississippi, to Chattanooga, Tennessee, by rail, and then joined Gen. E. Kirby Smith in a bold invasion of Kentucky. Checked at Perryville in October by Gen. D.C. Buell, Bragg retreated to Murfreesboro, Tennessee, where he fought a bloody battle against Gen. W.S. Rosecrans in late 1862 and early 1863. Rosecrans's Tullahoma Campaign in June 1863 compelled Bragg to abandon Tennessee, but after receiving Gen. James Longstreet's Corps from Virginia in September as reinforcements for the Battle of Chickamauga, he drove the Federals back into Chattanooga and began a siege that lasted until Gen. U.S. Grant arrived from Mississippi in November 1863 and drove the Confederates back into Georgia. Relieved of command of the Army of Tennessee, Bragg became President Davis's military adviser in February 1864. He exercised considerable power and served the president and the Confederacy well during the eight months he held this position, but his appointment came too late in the war for him to have a determinative impact. In January 1865, while still serving as the president's military adviser, Bragg engaged in his most ineffective performance as a field commander: he failed to prevent the Federals from taking Fort Fisher, which protected Wilmington, North Carolina, the last Confederate port open to blockade runners. Bragg spent the last weeks of the war under the command of Gen. J.E. Johnston attempting to check Gen. W.T. Sherman's advance. Bragg and his wife were part of the Confederate flight from Richmond until their capture in Georgia. Bragg, who lived in relative poverty after the war, died in Galveston, Texas, in 1876, and is buried in Mobile. Never a great field commander, he had talents the Confederacy needed but seldom used: the army possessed no better disciplinarian or drillmaster. An able organizer and administrator, he excelled as an inspector, possessed a good eye for strategy, and proved himself a dedicated patriot.

While President Davis worried about the future of his recently created country, he received an unexpected and unwelcome visitor. In early June, Maj. Gen. Sterling Price journeyed from Tupelo, Mississippi, to the capital to lobby for command of the Trans-Mississippi Department, which was still technically under Maj. Gen. Earl Van Dorn's authority. Price also demanded that his Missourians accompany him back across the Mississippi to spearhead a new campaign that he would lead to liberate his adopted state. The trip was one long victory parade for Price, who resurrected his old political skills at dinner parties and platform speeches along the way, capitalizing on his martial reputation garnered from victories

David Glasgow Farragut

Born in Tennessee in 1801. After moving with his family to New Orleans, Farragut came under the guardianship of Capt. David Porter. In 1810, not yet ten years old, he was appointed midshipman in the U.S. Navy. The following year he joined Porter's crew aboard the frigate USS *Essex*. He served in the Pacific during the War of 1812, and was appointed prize master of a captured British vessel. He was also actively engaged during Porter's defeat by two British warships at Valparaiso. He was taken prisoner and exchanged in November 1814. Farragut spent the next five years on duty mostly in the Mediterranean. He studied in Tunis and in 1825 became a lieutenant. Thereafter saw a variety of duties in the Gulf of Mexico and the south Atlantic. In 1841, he was promoted to commander and the following year took command of the sloop USS *Decatur*. Largely left out of the action during the Mexican War, Farragut was given command of the sloop USS *Saratoga* but arrived too late to participate in the capture of Veracruz. Varied assignments, and promotion to captain, followed, and at the outbreak of the Civil War, he was awaiting orders at his home in Norfolk, Virginia. He moved his family to

won in the previous year. Many influential western politicians supported his appointment, and some even speculated that he was a possible candidate for the presidency, if the South survived long enough to have the election or if an increasingly unpopular Davis was impeached. Price was recommended for the position by Van Dorn as well, as the Pea Ridge debacle had ended all his dreams of glory in the frontier theater of war.[7]

In Richmond, Price presented his petition personally to Davis, who requested a formal written submission of the application. Davis had little regard for the amateur solider whom he considered as "the vainest man I ever met," and had little patience for Price's numerous complaints over his transfer across the river. In a final meeting Davis announced that the

New York after Virginia's secession and was initially viewed with suspicion as a Southerner. His only assignment in 1861 was as a member of the retirement board. In January 1862, he became commander of the West Gulf Blockading Squadron with the mission of capturing New Orleans. The city fell in April 1862 after the bulk of Farragut's fleet ran past Forts Jackson and St. Philip on the Mississippi River and captured the defenseless city in what may have been the most decisive single action of the war—one from which the Confederate government could not rebound. Farragut was made rear admiral in June 1862 for this action. He moved his fleet up the Mississippi and, in July 1862, fought past the Vicksburg batteries before returning to the Gulf of Mexico. He again ascended the Mississippi to attack Port Hudson in March 1863. In July of that year, he returned to New York and received a hero's welcome. He returned to the Gulf in January 1864, and began preparing for operations against Mobile. In August 1864, Farragut launched an attack against Confederate forces in Mobile Bay by running past Forts Morgan and Gaines. While aboard his flagship, USS *Hartford*, he is reported to have exclaimed "Damn the torpedoes, full speed ahead" while leading the fleet beyond the forts and through a mine field. In December, suffering from poor health, he returned to New York, where citizens presented him with $50,000 for the purchase of a house in the city. He was promoted to vice admiral in December 1864. He returned to duty in the waning days of the war and was among the first Federal officers to enter Richmond after its fall. After the war he commanded the European Squadron and in July 1866 became the first full admiral in the nation's history. Admiral Farragut died at Portsmouth, New Hampshire, in 1870, still on active duty in his sixtieth year of service with the U.S. Navy.

post was already filled by Maj. Gen. John Magruder, and that the Missourians could not be spared from Mississippi at the moment. Price bristled at the rejection and exclaimed, "Well, Mr. President, if you will not let me serve you, I will nevertheless serve my *country*. You cannot prevent me from doing that." Price further declared that, "I will send you my resignation, and go back to Missouri and raise another army there without your assistance, and fight again under the flag of Missouri, and win new victories for the South in spite of the government." Davis responded sharply, "Your resignation will be promptly accepted, General; and if you do go back to Missouri and raise another army, and win victories for the South, or do it any service at all, no one will be more *pleased* than myself, or—more *surprised*."

Price retorted, "then I will surprise you, sir!" and struck the table before him with such force that it "set the inkstands and everything upon it a-dancing."[8]

Price immediately stormed out to write his resignation, which Davis returned the next day. The ex-governor was simply too popular with his troops and constituents to dismiss, and his removal might spark the downfall of Confederate support in the region. Price was informed by Davis that his men would be returned west of the Mississippi as soon it "could be safely done," and with that small token of appeasement, Price returned to the army.[9]

Van Dorn, freed from his Trans-Mississippi troubles, was subsequently assigned to command the Confederate defenses of Vicksburg, which were only twenty-seven miles from his birthplace in Port Gibson, Mississippi. Dedicated to driving the enemy from his native soil, and eager to remove the stain of defeat that had darkened his reputation ever since his earlier disaster in Arkansas, Van Dorn approached his new assignment with customary vigor and enthusiasm. Vicksburg was the next objective on the Federal itinerary along the Mississippi River, and when Van Dorn arrived on June 27, the city was in a state of ship-borne siege. It had been under continual bombardment for a week from Flag Officer David G. Farragut's flotilla of gunboats, which had steamed up from New Orleans, and Charles H. Davis's brown water navy, which floated down from Memphis. With an unbroken record of success on the "big muddy," the Federals felt that one more strike might open the entire Mississippi River to Federal navigation and split the Confederacy in half. In the struggle for supremacy on the river, no other location in the entire South was as vital as Vicksburg, and Van Dorn refused to let it fall without a fight. In an attempt to further assert his control of the region and eliminate a growing illicit cotton trade, Van Dorn declared martial law in the area under his authority, an act that won him no favors from the local press.[10]

The artillery-studded bluffs of Vicksburg proved to be more challenging than anything the Federal Navy had yet encountered during their aquatic conquest. When the blockade and bombardment proved ineffective, Union Brig. Gen. Thomas Williams resorted to digging a canal across a peninsula that would theoretically allow ships to bypass the fortifications, but the project accomplished little else other than the exhaustion of his men in the Louisiana swamps. Realizing that it would take a combined land and river assault to secure the stronghold, Farragut wrote to Halleck and requested aid from the Army. Halleck, still preoccupied with garrisoning Corinth and capturing Chattanooga, replied that "the scattered and weakened condition of my forces renders it impossible for me at the present moment to detach any to co-operate with you on Vicksburg." With this refusal, Halleck had once again missed a chance to deliver a decisive blow to the Confederacy, one that might have significantly shortened the war.[11]

On July 15 the Confederate ironclad *Arkansas*, recently completed on the Yazoo River, ran through the gauntlet of the thirty-seven ship Federal fleet in a thrilling battle, and survived to dock in Vicksburg. The daring venture proved to be the climactic display of defiance during Farragut's fruitless operation. Van Dorn and Vicksburg held out against the U.S. Navy, and Farragut gave up the endeavor on July 24 to return downriver to Baton Rouge.[12]

With the Federals in retreat, and his reputation partially repaired, Van Dorn instantly followed in pursuit. He sent five thousand men under Maj. Gen. John C. Breckinridge down the river, intending to reconquer the Louisiana state capital of Baton Rouge, and perhaps even retake New Orleans as well. But as he had done in Arkansas, Van Dorn launched his men into a demanding campaign without adequate reconnaissance or supplies, and soon heat, humidity, hunger, and mosquitoes inflicted more damage on the expedition than Union bullets. Within days, almost half of the men occupied hospital beds rather than the streets of Baton Rouge. The attack itself was a miserable failure and the *Arkansas*, which had been sent to reinforce Breckinridge, broke down and rather than surrendering the ship to the Union fleet, the captain ordered it destroyed.[13]

Nevertheless, Union Gen. Benjamin "Beast" Butler, whose troops were suffering from the climate as intensely as the Confederates, decided to abandon Baton Rogue and retreat to New Orleans. Southern troops reoccupied the city and fortified the bend of Port Hudson, securing the critical Red River supply line and extending Confederate control on the Mississippi. The campaign, despite its shortcomings, was still the most successful offensive thus far for Van Dorn, though the affair brought little solace to his ego.[14]

On July 14, Halleck received a wire from President Lincoln stating, "I am very anxious—almost impatient—to have you here." Halleck, nicknamed "Old Brains" for his intellectual capacity, was on his way to Washington to replace McClellan as general-in-chief of the Army. McClellan currently had his concentration focused on Robert E. Lee's vicious counterattacks outside of Richmond, and Lincoln needed Halleck's administrative talents to coordinate the various military efforts of the Union. After recovering from a bout of intestinal difficulties in June that he termed "the evacuation of Corinth," Halleck had little desire to enter the political squabbles of the nation's capital. In a wire to Sherman, Halleck complained "I have done my best to avoid it. I have studied out and can finish the campaign in the West. Don't understand and cannot manage affairs in the East. Moreover, do not want to have anything to do with the quarrels of Stanton and McClellan." Sherman replied with both reassurance and foresight, "I attach more importance to the West than the East. . . . The man who at the end of this war holds the military control of the Valley of the Mississippi will be the man."[15]

The departure of Halleck, regardless of his misgivings, was a beneficial turn of events for Grant. In the shuffling of generals, Grant was given command of the District of West Tennessee, which included northern Mississippi and the areas of Kentucky and Tennessee west of the Tennessee River. Grant had at his disposal the 38,485-man Army of the Tennessee, which he commanded personally, and the 25,224-man Army of the Mississippi, now under Rosecrans.[16]

Grant's forces were stretched thin along a 140-mile defensive front ranging from Cherokee, Alabama, all the way to Memphis. He lacked the manpower or resources to continue the subjugation of Mississippi, and was strained to maintain the territory already occupied. The squandering of the strategic initiative tried the patience of the ever aggressive Grant. "The most anxious period of the war, to me, was during the time the Army of the Tennessee was guarding the territory acquired by the fall of Corinth and Memphis and before I was sufficiently reinforced to take the offensive," he would later write.[17]

Grant set about improving the defenses of Corinth, which had been started by Beauregard in April. These ramparts covered the northern approaches to the city, and were some two and a half miles outside of town. Halleck added to the fortifications during his command of the city by building an inner line a mile and half from Corinth around the entirety of the crossroads. Grant considered the enterprise valuable, both to add to his soldiers' protection and to relieve their boredom, but Rosecrans felt the protective line was too extended for the reduced garrison to man effectively. While work continued on the "Halleck Line," Rosecrans put his engineer's eye to use and observed to Grant that "this line isn't worth much to us, because it is too long. We cannot occupy it." He suggested constructing a series of five batteries on high ground surrounding the town, connected by breastworks. Grant saw the merits of Rosecrans' suggestion, and soon Rosecrans was supervising the creation of the most formidable defensive works yet seen in the war.[18]

Throughout the early summer, a stalemate ensued as both sides continued to prepare their forces for the impending, inevitable clash of arms that would determine who would control northern Mississippi. Bragg's Confederate army lingered anxiously in Tupelo, while Union troops refitted, drilled, and sweated in the oppressive heat of the environment. Maj. Gen. William T. Sherman wrote that "the quiet of a New England Sabbath prevails." With disease and discomfort commonplace, one Federal solider wrote home that "our diet has been principally sow belly and magets [*sic*], bacon and crackers, some say the crackers have magets [*sic*] in them, but I don't look for them. All I can say is if they get between my teeth they will get hurt." A prolonged drought only worsened conditions, and rendered any operation dependent upon the availability of water supplies. The famed mineral springs in Iuka, a "pretty little village" named for a Chickasaw chief and a popular tourist attraction before the war, went dry. Grant wrote from Corinth in August that "reconnaissance far to the front shows the country to be so dry that an attack on this place is hardly to be apprehended."[19]

In late July the new Confederate commander in the West, Gen. Braxton Bragg, decided to attempt a bold and daring counterstrike. After realizing that a massive redeployment was possible, he transferred the majority of his army by rail east to reinforce Gen. Edmund Kirby Smith at Chattanooga. In a span of less than two weeks more than 30,000 men rode 776 miles over six railroads, from Tupelo down to Mobile, from Mobile to Montgomery and Atlanta, and finally north to Chattanooga. The sudden relocation of Bragg's base of operations was one of the first major uses of strategic rail transport in military history, and highlighted the invaluable worth of the railroads in sustaining the South's ability to wage war. The complicated venture was successful thanks to Bragg's meticulous planning and efficient execution, and came as a complete shock to the Federals. When combined with the 9,000 men already in

Chattanooga, the Confederates now had more than enough strength to repel Buell's slow-moving army, and after the southern raiders Nathan Bedford Forrest and John Hunt Morgan generated havoc with his supply lines, Buell withdrew back to Nashville.[20]

Buell's abrupt retreat left an open door to Kentucky, and Bragg soon began planning an invasion into the Union occupied slave state. This forward movement would challenge northern control of the Bluegrass region, and might induce thousands of disgruntled Kentuckians to join the Confederate Army. The campaign would disrupt Federal supply lines in the West, possibly forcing the abandonment of Nashville and Middle Tennessee. By rapid maneuvers Bragg hoped to reclaim the lost territory without firing a shot, and choose his own ground for battle somewhere north of the Tennessee line. In August, Bragg began moving troops up to Knoxville, marching hard for Louisville.[21]

The bold gamble demanded coordination and cooperation from the Confederate forces that stayed behind in Mississippi. While Bragg and Kirby Smith led the Confederate incursion into Kentucky, Price and Van Dorn remained in the Magnolia State. Price, now commanding the old "Army of the West" in Tupelo, had roughly 16,000 veterans in two divisions, while Van Dorn had nearly equal strength at Vicksburg. Bragg intended for the two to collaborate to prevent Grant and Rosecrans from reinforcing Buell, and to attack either Union force if the opportunity presented itself; neither Price nor Van Dorn had control over the other, however, and technically only Price was under Bragg's authority. Bragg outlined his optimistic intentions when he wrote that "Van Dorn and Price will advance simultaneously with us from Mississippi on West Tennessee, and I trust we may all unite in Ohio."[22]

Bragg and Price were complete contrasts in command style, a fact that did not improve their relationship. Bragg, a

West Point graduate and professional soldier, had a reputation as a stern disciplinarian while Price, the public servant turned soldier, was much more lenient with his men. A tale circulated throughout the ranks that a number of Price's Missourians had been caught stealing corn from a local farmer, and were lightly punished by Price. Bragg, when informed of the incident, consequently demanded that Price court martial and execute the men, whereupon Price abruptly replied that "his men were not to be shot for taking roasting-ears."[23]

Before he left for Chattanooga, Maj. Gen. William J. Hardee, commanding a wing in Bragg's army, warned Thomas Snead, the chief of staff in Price's District, to be wary of involvement in any of Van Dorn's "adventures." Hardee feared that Van Dorn would attempt to draw Price into some rash gamble with him, and bluntly declared "that the success of General Bragg's movement into Tennessee and Kentucky depends greatly upon his (Price's) ability to keep Grant from reinforcing Buell, and consequently that General Bragg would sternly disapprove the sending of any reinforcements whatever to Van Dorn." Price should be "ready to move northward at a moment's notice," to support Bragg, Hardee continued. Hardee soon proved to be a prophet, for when Van Dorn was asked by Price to combine their forces for an assault against Grant, he responded on August 11 that "it will be two weeks before I can do anything," and then requested a brigade to bail out Breckinridge's stalled Baton Rogue excursion.[24]

All throughout August these two commanders communicated back and forth, failing at every attempt of coordination. On August 2, Bragg wired Price that "the road is open for you into Western Tennessee," presuming that Grant had been severely weakened by the transfer of reinforcements to Buell, and proposing that the Missourian should boldly strike forth alone against the enemy. But Bragg was misinformed. Both Grant and Rosecrans remained together, too strong for Price to fight without the assistance of "the defender of Vicksburg."[25]

Disappointed with the relative inaction in Mississippi, Bragg then instructed Price to "not depend much on Van Dorn; he has his hands full," and later wrote in the same month that "we shall confidently expect to meet you on the Ohio and there open the way to Missouri," capitalizing on "Old Pap's" outspoken desire to return home. But Van Dorn was still not ready to move as September approached, and Price felt he had no other option but to wait and prepare his men for the long-anticipated upcoming battle, whenever it may occur. He gathered supplies, drilled his army into prime condition, and sent his cavalry raiding into Tennessee to keep Grant occupied and to gather intelligence.[26]

As the summer progressed, southern hopes were raised with a series of remarkable victories. In the East, Robert E. Lee drove McClellan back from Richmond in the Seven Days campaign in July, and in late August, Lee thrashed John Pope, who had left Corinth for Virginia, at the Battle of Second Manassas. While Bragg and Kirby Smith marched into Kentucky and Price and Van Dorn bickered in Mississippi, Lee was planning to carry the war northward out of his native state. In early September the Army of Northern Virginia crossed the Potomac River and invaded Maryland in an attempt to disrupt Federal supply and communication lines. Similar to Bragg in Kentucky, Lee hoped that a strong Confederate presence in a border slave state would motivate the native population to rise up en masse against northern occupation. A thrust that threatened Pennsylvania, while a second threatened Ohio, together might create panic across the North, and hopefully produce favorable results in the November congressional elections. The momentum of the war had shifted South.[27]

Across the Confederacy, from the "Atlantic to the Territories," soldiers in gray were on the offensive in tandem, in the first and only such operation they ever attempted. The most dramatic strategic reversal in American military history occurred in that hot, bloody summer of 1862. In late May, the Confederacy seemed to be on the brink of total defeat, and only three short months later, it appeared to be on the verge of total victory. Success in either of the audacious invasions might provoke European recognition of the southern republic, and instigate foreign intervention to force the North to sign a peace treaty granting independence to the South. To many, the end of the war was nearly in sight.[28]

While Price and Van Dorn wired and wrangled, Grant and Rosecrans watched and waited. In late July, Rosecrans reported that the Confederates felt that "with Bragg on the east and Price in the center, as they say, the Yankees will be made to skedaddle." Rosecrans's information was gathered by a young cavalry colonel named Philip Sheridan, who had captured a substantial amount of Confederate dispatches. Rosecrans thereafter wrote to Halleck that Sheridan "is worth his weight in gold" and recommended him for promotion. By early September, Halleck had detached three divisions from the Army of the Mississippi to reinforce Buell, leaving Grant only fifty thousand men to defeat any Confederate advance and combat the eternally troublesome guerillas. On September 9, Rosecrans discovered from a paroled prisoner that Price had been in Tupelo, reassuring citizens that complained of Yankee depredations that he "would rectify matters in a week or two."[29]

Rosecrans's intelligence was accurate. Finally, after receiving explicit orders from Bragg and obtaining no sign of support from Van Dorn, Price decided to strike at the Union outpost of Iuka. Price believed, as Bragg had informed him, that Rosecrans was crossing the Tennessee River to relocate to Nashville, but "Old Rosy" had actually remained in Northeast Mississippi. On September 11, Price moved out from Baldwyn towards Iuka, taking a route which would allow him to threaten the Union Tennessee River supply depot of Eastport. The course also enabled Price to cross the river if he found favorable prospects in Middle Tennessee. Iuka was held by one

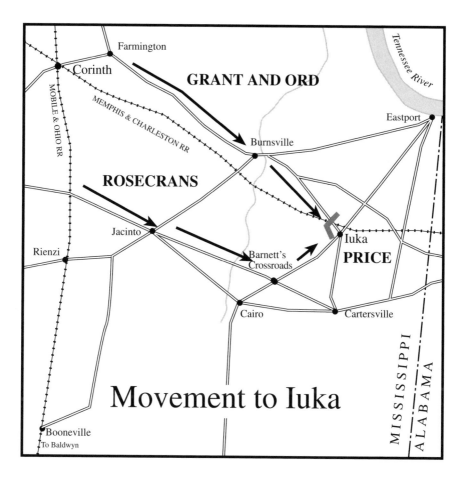

Movement to Iuka

Federal brigade under Col. Robert Murphy, who quickly evacuated the town when he discovered the entire Army of the West
bearing down on him.[30]

During the night of September 14, the Confederates began
a forced march in order to reach Iuka before Murphy and his
brigade could realize they were being targeted. Price drove his
men the last three miles at the quick time, which challenged
the endurance of his exhausted and footsore soldiers. One
Texan later recollected the march, "thirty inches at a step and
116 steps per minute; practically it meant for us to get over

that piece of road as rapidly as our tired legs could carry us. To keep up with this march was the supreme effort of the expedition on my part."[31]

The exhausted men arrived to find that the Union troops gone, but they had left behind a considerable prize. Murphy had no time to burn the massive quantities of supplies amassed in Iuka, and the Confederates stumbled upon what one Missourian described as a "perfect El Dorado of supplies." Instantly the half-starved soldiers fell upon the provisions, a feast compared to their typical fare of "Beef & Baker's Bread." One amazed soldier in gray wrote home of the bonanza, and of the incredible inadequacy of Confederate logistics, that "the Yankees had everything there and I know most of their troops live better in the army than they do at home. . . . Imagination can hardly conceive how well *their armies* are supplied and how poorly *ours*." One hungry Southerner was thrilled to discover a large resort hotel in Iuka where "every room was filled with cheese and crackers, hams and hominy and molasses and whiskey." The memorable consumption was followed by the first real rest the men had had in days.[32]

Now that Price had marched out into the open, Grant saw his chance to regain the initiative in northern Mississippi and strike the exposed Confederates. Halleck gave Grant clear orders and instructed him to "do everything in your power to prevent Price from crossing the Tennessee River. A junction of Price and Bragg in Tennessee or Kentucky would be most disastrous. They should be fought while separate." Grant agreed with Halleck's assertions and replied, "I will do all in my power to prevent such a catastrophe." Grant was good to his word, and quickly prepared a trap to destroy Price.[33]

After months of enduring the bitterness and disgrace of his near-disaster at Shiloh, and waiting patiently for an opportunity for redemption to present itself, Grant at last had a chance to deliver a decisive blow against the enemy. He would leave a sufficient number of men in Corinth to guard against any move

Painting of a Confederate camp near Corinth, May 10, 1862, by Conrad Chapman of the 3d Kentucky Infantry. *Library of Congress.*

Van Dorn might make, and take fifteen thousand men to Iuka to face Price. Maj. Gen. Edward O.C. Ord would lead six thousand men west from Burnsville, Mississippi, to focus Price's attention, while Rosecrans marched from Jacinto, Mississippi, with nine thousand Federals in a flanking assault from the south, closing the noose around Price's neck in a classic pincer movement. It was a dangerous and complex proposition to undertake, riskier than any Grant had yet attempted. If Price fell upon either of the Union columns with his whole Confederate force, Union troops could be quickly overwhelmed before reinforcements could come to their aid. The attack would depend on speed, stealth, surprise, and a healthy dose of luck. But if the two separate Federal movements could be successfully coordinated, Price would be left with nowhere to escape. If all went as planned, the Army of the West would be destroyed.[34]

3

"THE HARDEST-FOUGHT FIGHT WHICH I HAVE EVER WITNESSED"

Maj. Gen. Ulysses S. Grant's battle plan for Iuka was straightforward in conception but intricate in execution. To close the trap, Brig. Gen. William S. Rosecrans's column would advance eastward to Barnett's Crossroads, and then turn northward along the Jacinto and Fulton roads to Iuka, while Maj. Gen. Edward O.C. Ord's forces blocked the Burnsville road six miles northwest of the town. Confederate Maj. Gen. Sterling Price, whom Rosecrans had equated with an "old woodpecker" for his wily nature, would be boxed into a corner with the Tennessee River at his back, blocking any escape. Grant would remain in Burnsville overseeing Ord's detachment, where he could maintain communications with Rosecrans by courier. Railcars would be standing ready to rush reinforcements back to Corinth if Confederate Maj. Gen. Earl Van Dorn should attempt another impetuous advance while Grant dealt with Price. Unfortunately for the Union forces, twenty-seven miles of bad road and four to six hours would separate dispatches between Rosecrans and Ord until they reunited, which complicated the operation significantly.[1]

Grant intended for Rosecrans to attack in conjunction with Ord at dawn on September 19. Rosecrans's component consisted of his two divisions of the Army of the Mississippi, led by brigadier generals David Stanley and Charles Hamilton. Both men were West Pointers, and it was Hamilton who had initially proposed the flanking assault Grant was now enacting. The Federal troops marched out with optimistic expectations of success, but many still harbored doubts about Grant's enduring reputation for being surprised on the battlefield due to heavy drinking. Prior to the campaign a Minnesota artilleryman wrote home describing General Ord as "the old fellow looks just like a Russian Marshal with his fierce Mustachios and beard. I would have a great deal more confidence in him than in Grant."[2]

Almost immediately, the synchronization of the two wings began to breakdown. After midnight, Grant received a dispatch from Rosecrans informing him that unexpected delays would postpone his arrival until "1 or 2 o'clock" the next afternoon, extinguishing any hope of a coordinated sunrise assault. A native guide, either intentionally or unintentionally, had misled Stanley's division down the wrong road, costing Rosecrans five precious hours. Grant, considering the poor condition of the roads, doubted that Rosecrans would reach Iuka by the time anticipated. He therefore ordered Ord to move forward and engage Price's pickets to occupy the Missourian's attention, but to delay his assault until Rosecrans appeared or he heard the sounds of "firing to the south." Grant's dispatch containing this essential alteration in his strategy was somehow lost in the thick tangle of trees, swamps, and undergrowth of Tishomingo County and never reached Rosecrans.[3]

EDWARD O.C. ORD

Born in Maryland in 1818, Ord was appointed to U.S. Military Academy at age sixteen, and graduated seventeenth out of thirty-one cadets in 1839. Brevetted 2d lieutenant in 3rd Artillery, he served in the Second Seminole War, and was promoted to 1st lieutenant for his service there. During the Mexican War, Ord was stationed in California. He afterwards served at

numerous frontier posts. In 1859, he was at the artillery school at Fort Monroe, Virginia, during John Brown's raid on Harper's Ferry and participated in the expedition that captured Brown. He was captain of the 3rd Artillery when war broke out, and in September 1861 was promoted to brigadier general of volunteers. Given command of a brigade in George McCall's division of "Pennsylvania Reserves," he saw his first action at Dranesville in December 1861. Ord transferred to divisional command in Irwin McDowell's corps and on May 3, 1862, was promoted to major general and reassigned to the Western Theater. He participated in the Corinth campaign and was severely wounded in action near Pocahontas, Mississippi. He returned to duty during the siege of Vicksburg in June 1863 as commander of XIII Corps, and led his corps through the Jackson Campaign. In spring of 1864, he returned to the Eastern Theater and was given command of VIII Corps during the siege of Petersburg. Soon afterwards, he was transferred to command of the XVIII Corps, which led an assault on Fort Harrison in September 1864 where he was seriously wounded. He recovered and in January 1865 replaced Benjamin Butler as commander of the Army of the James and Department of North Carolina. He remained in this position until the surrender at Appomattox. After the war Ord stayed in the army, retiring as a major general in 1881. In 1883, while on a trip to Vera Cruz, he contracted yellow fever and died in Havana on July 22. He is buried in Arlington National Cemetery.

While Rosecrans pressed on through a "wild and uncultivated country," Grant attempted an unorthodox ruse to ensnare Price without firing a shot. During the night of September 18, Grant received a wire containing the first wildly inaccurate reports of the battle of Antietam, which had been fought the previous day in Maryland. The message stated the startling news that "Longstreet and his entire division prisoners. General Hill killed. Entire rebel army of Virginia destroyed." Grant forwarded the note through Ord to Price, asking him to "avoid the useless bloodshed and lay down his arms," with an endorsement that "the dispatch is reliable." Ord conveyed the message across the lines, adding, "I think this battle decides the war finally. . . . There is not the slightest doubt of the truth of the dispatch in my mind."[4]

Not surprisingly, Price considered the request an "insolent demand" and responded with an emphatic refusal. He firmly informed Ord that if the information was accurate, which he did not believe, then it "would only move him and his soldiers to greater exertions in behalf of their country, and that neither he nor they will ever lay down their arms . . . until the independence of the Confederate States shall have been acknowledged by the United States." If Grant hoped to repeat his Donelson triumph and capture another large Confederate army, his soldiers would have to earn it on the battlefield.[5]

On the morning of September 19, Price received two couriers from Van Dorn which informed the general that the "defender of Vicksburg" was finally prepared for a long overdue coordinated movement against the Federals. The dispatch also notified Price that he was now once again under Van Dorn's command, which "Old Pap" accepted without protest. Price realized that a joint operation would be required to regain control of northern Mississippi, and as Van Dorn held seniority, the assault would be under his direction. To clarify his authority, Van Dorn wrote to the secretary of war, "I ought to have command of the movements of Price, that there may be concert of action." President Davis, quite tired of the continual inaction in his native state, intervened and replied, "Your troops must cooperate, and can only do so by having one head.

Lewis Henry Little

Born in 1817 in Baltimore, Little was commissioned as a 2nd lieutenant in the Army in 1839 without the customary West Point education, most likely due to the fact that his father was veteran of the War of 1812 and a congressman from Maryland. Little served with the 7th Infantry in the Mexican War and was brevetted captain for bravery at the Battle of Monterrey. In August 1847, he was officially promoted to captain, and remained in the Army after the war, serving on various frontier posts and accompanying Albert Sidney Johnston's expedition to Utah during the 1858 Mormon Conflict. When the secession crisis erupted, Little was stationed in Missouri, where after resigning he became a colonel in Sterling Price's Missouri State Guard. Little became the commander of the 1st Missouri Brigade in November 1861, which he led with distinction at Pea Ridge in March 1862. In April of that same year he was promoted to brigadier general and in June received command of a division in the Army of the West. Although sick with fever, he led his division to Iuka, where he was killed instantly in the early stages of the battle when a bullet struck him in the forehead. During the night, Little was buried in a hastily dug grave in Iuka, but after the war his body was disinterred and reburied in the Green Mount Cemetery in Baltimore. Although highly regarded by his fellow officers and his commander Price, who considered him his most trusted subordinate, Little's untimely death prevented his full potential as a commander from being realized.

Your rank makes you the commander, and such I suppose were the instructions of General Bragg."[6]

In Iuka it was now clear that Rosecrans had not crossed the Tennessee River, but was instead stationed to prevent a Confederate crossing. On the 20th, Price began to load his wagons and prepared his command to evacuate the town and retreat southward to Baldwyn. His two divisions, led by brigadier generals Dabney Herndon Maury and Lewis Henry Little, maintained their defensive positions northwest of town. Little, a Maryland-born Mexican War veteran who had served with the Army of the West since the beginning of the war, was Price's most trusted subordinate. At 2:30 in the afternoon Price received word of a large Union force drawing up on him from the south. He immediately ordered his only reserve, Brig. Gen. Louis Hébert's brigade of Little's division, to investigate the suspicious movement on the double quick.[7]

In the meantime, Rosecrans's troops had been on the march since sunrise to make up lost time, unaware that Grant had delayed Ord's attack. While in route Rosecrans sent an optimistic message to Grant, "eighteen miles to Iuka, but think I shall make it by the time mentioned. . . . If Price is there he will have become well engaged by time we come up, and if so twenty regiments and thirty pieces cannon will finish him." By noon he had reached Barnett's Crossroads, the critical road junction where he planned to divide his forces in half, sending one division up the Jacinto Road and the other along the Fulton Road in an effort to trap Price. But reconnaissance showed that the roads were separated by five miles of impenetrable swamp, preventing either division from communication or support from the other. Confronted with this new information, Rosecrans modified his line of approach. He decided to march his entire column up the Jacinto Road, then cut off the Fulton Road by capturing Iuka and denying the Confederates any chance of escape.[8]

This tactical adjustment would be safer and easier to execute, so long as Grant kept Price's attention diverted from his left flank. If Rosecrans failed in his calculated venture, however, the Fulton Road would be left wide open for Price's planned withdrawal. Satisfied with his arrangements, Rosecrans ordered Colonel Sanborn's brigade of Hamilton's division to lead the way. Curiously, "Old Rosy" failed to communicate his decision with headquarters, and Grant was not aware of the variation in his plan until the next morning.[9]

The Federal Army of the Mississippi had encountered little resistance thus far in its perilous undertaking, except a brief

CHARLES HAMILTON

Born in 1822 in Westernville, New York, Hamilton attended the Aurora Academy and was appointed to the United States Military Academy in 1839. He graduated twenty-sixth in the class of 1843, while his classmate U.S. Grant graduated twenty-first. During the Mexican War, Hamilton survived a serious wound at the Battle of Molino del Rey and was promoted to the regular rank of 1st lieutenant and brevetted captain for gallantry. After the war he endured the monotony of frontier service before resigning his commission in 1853 to settle on a farm in Wisconsin, where he manufactured flour. When Fort Sumter was fired upon, he offered his services to his state and was commissioned colonel of the 3rd Wisconsin Infantry, and shortly thereafter was promoted to brigadier general. In early 1862, Hamilton served in the Shenandoah Valley and was given command of a division in the III Corps, Army of the Potomac, during the Peninsula Campaign. On April 30, after the siege of Yorktown, he was removed from command by Gen. George McClellan and reassigned to the West, where Hamilton led a division in William S. Rosecrans's army in the battles of Iuka and Corinth. Thanks to his friendship with Grant, he was promoted to major general to date from September 19, 1862, but soon became engaged in a political campaign in order to gain command of the XVII Corps, which led to his forced resignation on April 13, 1863. Returning to Wisconsin, he began farming again and in 1869 was appointed United States Marshal in Milwaukee by then President Grant. Hamilton later became involved in linseed oil production and served as president of the Hamilton Paper Company, as well as serving as a member and later president of the Board of Regents for the University of Wisconsin. He also commanded the Wisconsin department of the Military Order of the Loyal Legion, and found time to maintain a life-long feud with Rosecrans over their actions during Iuka and Corinth. Charles Hamilton died on April 17, 1891, and is buried in the Forest Home Cemetery in Milwaukee.

skirmish with the 1st Mississippi Partisan Rangers. As Hamilton advanced up the Jacinto Road, the cavalry screening his advance ran into a band of mounted Confederates, who fell back in a running battle. When the Bluecoats began crossing

Crippled Deer Creek, Confederate sharpshooters opened fire from the nearby home of a Mrs. Moore. General Hamilton, while observing the progress of the march, attracted the Southerners' attention, and a member of his escort fell dead from a sniper's bullet. After a short struggle, the gray horsemen were forced back, and Hamilton ordered the house burned in retaliation. As one Yankee dryly noted, "some person soon started a chemical process into operation which reduced the most of the material composing Mrs. Mooer's house into its original elements." As the column resumed the march through the clouds of black smoke and heat from the blazing structure, the skirmish continued, and soon the Union advance swept away Price's pickets. At 4:00 P.M. Sanborn's lead elements reached the crest of a ridge overgrown with underbrush only one mile from Iuka and halted in surprise. They had stumbled across a battle line of Confederate infantry.[10]

Blocking Rosecrans were the veterans of Hébert's brigade, who had arrived out of breath after rushing southward to the hill on the double quick. Directly in front of their position the ground descended swiftly into a deep, densely forested ravine, and then rose up into the brushwood ridge that Sanborn's men had just occupied. Hébert ordered two guns from the Clark Missouri Battery along the hill to probe the Federals, but they were soon driven back by skirmishers from the Federal 26th Missouri Infantry. Hébert countered by sending the 3rd Texas Cavalry (Dismounted) down into the ravine in a skirmish line to push back the troublesome Northerners. These Texans had been separated from their saddles in April when Van Dorn crossed the Mississippi River, due to a lack of watercraft to carry their horses across the river and a significant shortage of foot soldiers. Still bitter over their transfer to the infantry, the Texans entered their first major dismounted combat poorly prepared for the experience. The men had received only a limited amount of drill instruction, and some were still armed with their old double barreled shotguns, useless at any distance other than point-blank range.[11]

LOUIS HÉBERT

Born in Iberville Parish, Louisiana, in 1820, Hébert was the son of a prosperous sugar plantation owner. After completing his primary education with private tutors, he attended Jefferson College and earned an appointment to the United States Military Academy, from which he graduated in 1845, third out of a class of forty-one. In 1846, he resigned his commission to help his ailing

father manage the family plantation, but resumed his military profession as a major and later colonel in the state militia. In 1853, Hébert was elected to the state senate and was later appointed as Louisiana's chief engineer. He was serving on the Board of Public Works when secession occurred. Hébert was elected colonel of the 3rd Louisiana Infantry, which quickly garnered a reputation as being one of the best trained and hardest fighting regiments in the Western Theater. Ordered to Missouri in 1861, Hébert and his Louisianans won praise for their prominent role at Wilson's Creek, after which he was given command of a brigade under Sterling Price. While leading an unsuccessful attack at Pea Ridge on March 7, 1862, Hébert was surrounded and captured with a number of his men. After being exchanged, he returned to the army and was promoted to brigadier general on May 26, 1862. In September 1862, he led his reorganized brigade into furious fighting at Iuka, assuming command of the division when its commander, Brig. Gen. Henry Little, was killed. Hébert continued to command the division at the Battle of Corinth in October, where he performed effectively on the first day of battle, but mysteriously reported himself ill before the final assault on the second day, for reasons that are still unclear. After Corinth he returned to brigade command and served with distinction throughout the Vicksburg Campaign. After the surrender of the garrison in Vicksburg, he was once again exchanged and transferred to North Carolina, where he oversaw the heavy artillery around Fort Fisher and served as Chief Engineer of the Department of North Carolina until the end of the war. In the postwar years, Hébert returned to his home state of Louisiana, where he edited a newspaper and taught at private schools in Iberville and St. Martin Parishes. He died on January 7, 1901, and was buried Breaux Brigade, Louisiana. Aside from the second day of Corinth, Louis Hébert had a solid record of tactical leadership throughout the war. Interestingly, he was the first cousin of Confederate Brig. Gen. Paul O. Hébert and a brother-in-law of Confederate Brig. Gen. Walther H. Stevens.

As the ex-cavalrymen plunged down into the trees, one officer asked Hébert, "General, must we fix bayonets?" The excited Creole quickly responded, "Yes sir! What for you have ze bayonet, if you no fix him? Yes, by gar; fix him! Fix him!" The few Texans equipped with bayonets promptly obeyed and quickly drove the Federals back. The Texans' success allowed the Clark Battery to return, with two guns placed on the hill and the remaining two a short distance to the right of the Jacinto Road. Its commander, Lt. James L. Faris, immediately began dropping case shot and canister rounds on the Union battle line now forming on the ridge. Hébert then deployed the rest of his brigade. He first placed the 1st Texas Legion, another dismounted and disgruntled regiment, on the hill west of the road, then ordered the 14th and 17th Arkansas Consolidated Infantry to their left, and the 3rd Louisiana to the left flank.[12]

In reserve he held the 40th Mississippi, a green and rather peculiar outfit. The officers of the regiment had acquired a camel to haul their baggage, which was so immense that one private of the 3rd Texas speculated they had "brought about all their household goods along." He also commented that the unit contained "the tallest man and the largest boy in the army," the former stacking up to about "seven feet high" and the latter weighing in at "more than three hundred pounds." Capt. William E. Dawson's St. Louis Artillery was posted on the left of the Mississippians, to protect the left flank against any Federal incursions. Contented with his configuration, Hébert then paused to see what he was up against.[13]

On the ridge across the ravine, Hamilton hurriedly ordered his soldiers in blue into line to face the unexpected Southerners. The 5th Iowa of Sanborn's brigade was at the head of the column, and moved into the forest on the right of the Jacinto Road. To the left of the 5th Iowa, Hamilton positioned the unproven 48th Indiana and 4th Minnesota. The 26th Missouri, after being chased out of the ravine by the 3rd Texas, was thrown in to support the 5th Iowa on the right flank.

Sanborn held his final and most experienced regiment, the 16th Iowa, as a reserve in the center of the brigade. Hamilton directed the six guns of the 11th Battery, Ohio Light Artillery, to the crown of the ridge between the 5th Iowa and 48th Indiana and unlimbered on both sides of the road. Sanborn's men had served reliably from Island No. 10 to the siege of Corinth, but nothing the soldiers had endured prepared them for the carnage they would confront after a long, exhausting march of twenty miles. As Sanborn's 2,200 men prepared their defenses, General Rosecrans rode up to the ridge.[14]

Rosecrans instantly realized the seriousness of the threat he faced. After acquainting himself with Hamilton's formation, Rosecrans dispatched a battalion of the 3rd Michigan Cavalry along the Mill Road to investigate the possibilities of reaching the Fulton Road from an alternative route. Fortunately for Price, Hébert's brigade had arrived in the nick of time to save the Confederates last remaining escape route. Rosecrans was frustrated at not seizing his objective, but more disturbing was the fact that he had failed to hear any sounds of battle from the north while on the march. Suddenly, he found himself confronted by a large and aggressive element of the Army of the West, which was obviously not "well engaged" with Grant. Rather than closing a trap, Rosecrans faced the real possibility that he had unintentionally wandered into one.[15]

As Rosecrans's concerns mounted, he contacted Brig. Gen. Jeremiah Sullivan and ordered him to detach a contingent to guard the Settlement Road, which branched off the Jacinto Road near Sanborn's left flank. Sullivan dispatched the 10th Iowa and a section of the 12th Battery, Wisconsin Light Artillery, which fell into line on the left of the 4th Minnesota. Sullivan then situated the 10th Missouri to further protect the right flank, and held the remainder of his brigade, the 17th Iowa and 80th Ohio, in reserve. Sullivan's brigade roughly doubled the number of Union soldiers defending the ridge. Hamilton gave Sanborn command of the regiments to the left

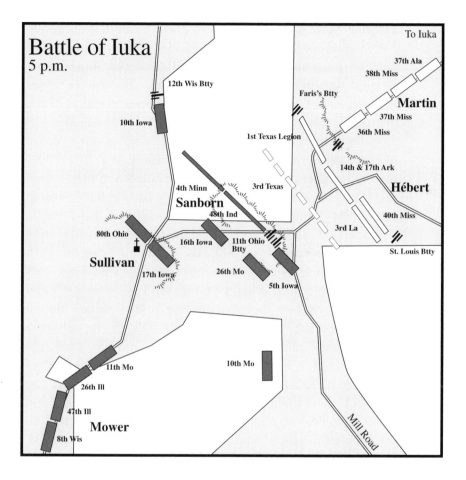

of the Jacinto Road, and placed Sullivan in charge of those to the right.[16]

Across the ravine, Hébert had hesitated to attack the ridge with his lone brigade, as he was unaware of the number of Federals that were arrayed against him and how many might be hidden beyond the rise. His artillery continued to fire, inflicting substantial damage on the Union troops, and he prudently reinforced the 3rd Texas skirmishers in the ravine with a company from the 3rd Louisiana. This short interval gave the Federals time to deploy Hamilton's division fully, and partially arrange their defense. An immediate assault would have caught Sanborn's brigade unprepared, still stacked up in marching formation along the Jacinto Road. Years later General Hamilton wrote that "their delay . . . was our salvation. An earlier attack would have enveloped the head of the column, and brought a disastrous rout."[17]

Soon swirling dust clouds announced the sprinting arrival of Confederate Col. John D. Martin's brigade, sent by Price to reinforce Hébert. Price had also sent General Little to take tactical command, to be closely followed by "Old Pap" himself. Little divided Martin's brigade in two, sending Colonel Martin with the 37th Alabama and 36th Mississippi to extend Hébert's left flank, while he personally led the 37th and 38th Mississippi on the right. It was now 5 P.M., and sunset was only an hour away, with twilight lasting until between 6:45 and 7:00. Little realized that daylight was rapidly fading, and he must act fast if he was to act at all. At 5:15 P.M., he ordered a general assault along the entire line.[18]

More than 3,300 Confederates, comprising one half of Little's division, advanced in two battle lines down the hill into the deep and darkening ravine. Smoke from the artillery and small arms fire settled into the trees of the gorge, further limiting visibility. As the mass of gray and butternut approached, the 3rd Texas reformed and fell in alongside on the left of the Texas Legion, compelling the Arkansans to join the following line. Confederate cannon quickly ceased firing to avoid endangering the advancing brigades and withdrew out of Union counter-battery range. As the line reached the edge of the ridge, one Texan later recalled that, "charge!' was the next command uttered by the brave little creole Herbert, and the Confederates, yelling like demons reveling in a saturnalia of death, pushed forward at the top of their speed."[19]

Lt. Cyrus Sears, commanding the 11th Ohio Battery, watched the enemy approach and patiently waited for the order to fire. A sergeant exclaimed, "By God, I guess we're going to let them gobble the whole damned shooting match before we strike a lick." A corporal responded, "I guess we are obeying orders." The sergeant countered furiously, "Damn the orders! To wait for orders at a time like this!" Sears could wait no longer. "With canister, aim low, and give them hell as fast as you can!" he shouted.[20]

The six guns erupted into a hail of canister, cutting down scores of Southerners. A member of the 3rd Texas vividly described the terrible devastation years afterwards: "I can never forget that moment—it came like lightening from a clear sky. The roaring of artillery, the rattle of musketry, the hailstorm of grape and ball were mowing us down like grain before we could locate from whence it came." As the assault continued, the Texans stalled in front of the Federal line. The Texan continued, "We were trapped; there could be no retreat, and certain death was in our advance. We fell prostrate on the ground. Captain Green, of Company I, arose on his knees and as he said, 'Steady, boys, steady,' he was decapitated by a cannon ball." The Union artillery was viciously effective at close range. "Lieutenant Ingram arose to stop one of the men from retreating, and he and the private were both cut in two with grapeshot. Our ranks were shattered in the twinkling of an eye," the Texan finished.[21]

Sears's battery was the centerpiece of the Federal line, and it soon became the focal point of the Confederate onslaught. To the left of the cannons, the seasoned 1st Texas Legion and 3rd Texas attacked the inexperienced 48th Indiana, who were already unnerved by severe Confederate artillery. The two Texas regiments, hidden from the Indianans as they crossed the ravine, emerged from the smoky abyss with a fury, delivering a devastating volley as they charged up the ridge. Shaken by the deadly shower of lead, the Indianans began to panic. Sanborn personally attempted to rally the regiment, and when the soldiers ignored his efforts, he shot two of them dead with a pistol. The 48th's colonel, Norman Eddy, made a noble effort to restore order but was severely wounded by a bullet. Without a leader, the Indianans disintegrated and began running for the rear. The 16th Iowa, posted as reserve behind the 48th, hastily fired into the mass of fleeing Federals and pursing Southerners, unintentionally creating more Union casualties than Confederate. Sanborn led the Iowans forward in a determined charge that drove the Texans back, but as the Union force crested the ridge, their commander, Col. Alexander Chambers, was shot from his horse. Like the Indianans, the Iowans quickly left the battle, never to return.[22]

The Texans ran into their own difficulties in the darkening smoke-haze of twilight. In the confusion of the attack, the Legion accidentally fired a volley into the backs of the 3rd Texas. On the other side of Sears's battery, the 5th Iowa was holding its own against vicious assaults from the 3rd Louisiana and the 14th and 17th Arkansas. A desperate standoff ensued, until the Iowans charged and drove the Confederates back down the ridge. The Southerners tried again, only to be driven back in another counterattack. The breakdown of the Indianans allowed the Texans to flank the Iowans and pour an appallingly effective enfilade fire upon their left. Four companies from the 26th Missouri were rushed in to support the 5th Iowa, but the Missourians were driven back after a brief but bloody stand. The 5th Iowa, after losing nearly half its men and depleting its ammunition, had to withdraw.[23]

On the Federal left, the 4th Minnesota remained intact in its original position, but was pinned down under vigorous enemy fire. The collapse of their infantry support left Sears's 11th Ohio battery in dire straits. Working their guns feverishly, the remaining men poured double canister into the Confederate line as fast as humanly possible. Without the protection of Springfield rifles, the battery became the vortex of death on the battlefield. Henry Neil, one of the battery's officers, acutely remembered the intense combat, "Cannoneers were falling. Other cannoneers coolly took their places and performed double duty. Drivers left their dead horses and took the places of dead or wounded comrades, only to be struck down in turn. Of the eighty horses only three remained standing and a withdrawal of the guns was impossible." Neil summed up the extreme circumstance the men faced by remarking "We had to fight first and think afterward."[24]

A vicious hand-to-hand struggle raged around the six cannons, as the Legion and the 3rd Texas charged the battery. One Texan described the carnage as "sword and bayonet were crossed. Muskets, revolvers, knives, ramrods, gun swabs—all mingled in the death-dealing fray. All the furies of torment seemed turned loose in that smoke-blinding boom of cannon and rattle of musketry." Sears reported the struggle to be an "all-absorbing handspike-and-ramrod, rough-and-tumble, devil take the hindmost fight." After a furious melee, in which several men of the battery were bayoneted, the Federals yielded the cannons. Sears managed to escape after spiking three of his guns, but his battery was annihilated. Neil reported that "the battery entered the fight with ninety-seven men and five officers, commissioned and acting. Of these, eighteen were killed and thirty-nine wounded, many mortally. . . . Of the cannoneers alone, forty-six were killed or wounded. Forty-six out of a total of fifty-four. More than five men out of every six." The 11th Ohio had suffered the worst loss of any light battery during the entire war at Iuka.[25]

During Hébert's assault, Price arrived to view the battle in person. At about 5:45 P.M., he ordered Little to deploy his other two brigades to crush the remaining Federals. As Price gestured, a bullet passed between his extended arms and entered Little's brain, killing him instantly. Price dismounted and broke into tears, grieving over Little's body "as he would for a son." Price ordered the slain general to be carried back to Iuka and informed Hébert that he was now in command of the division. The sudden loss of the "right arm of Price" threw

The death of Brig. Gen. Henry Little. *Ephraim Anderson's Memoirs: Historical and Personal.*

the Confederate command structure into chaos, and the confusion generated by Little's death probably prevented the total defeat of Hamilton's division. Little had been directing the 37th and 38th Mississippi against the Union left flank, but without his guidance, the attack went nowhere. The 38th Mississippi advanced until its colonel mysteriously received an order to halt and pull back. When the regiment began moving again, it was too dark to accomplish anything. The 37th Mississippi did manage to advance, but stumbled directly into the muskets of the 10th Iowa. After being thrown back by a surprise volley fired as they were crossing a fence into an open field, the Mississippians reformed and fought until dark against the Iowans and two guns from the 12th Wisconsin Battery, gaining little but casualties.[26]

After the capture of 11th Ohio Battery, General Sullivan deployed his last reserves, the 17th Iowa and the 80th Ohio, to retake the guns. The 80th Ohio wandered through the smoke straight into a Confederate ambush. A sharp fire fight occurred, but the Ohioans made no progress. The 17th Iowa, another green regiment, lost their colonel when his horse threw him, and the regiment soon came under an intense fire that caused the men to fall back. When the 17th Iowa advanced again, the soldiers entered a crossfire between Union and Confederate regiments, which "caused a dreadful stampede among the men, and all commenced firing in all directions without regard to where their guns were aimed."[27]

Sullivan managed to rally a sizable force from the various disorganized Union regiments and mounted a successful counterattack up the ridge. The Confederates reformed and pushed the mix of Federals back, only to lose the position a second time. At this point, the 14th and 17th Arkansas arrived, tipping the balance in favor of the South and driving off Sullivan's exhausted soldiers. Thomas Abbott, a member of the 17th Arkansas, later wrote of the fierce nature of the fighting, remarking that "we pushed on so near the enemy that in the last shot which was fired the blaze of our guns met."[28]

In a final effort, Rosecrans sent the 11th Missouri from Mower's Brigade of Stanley's division up the ridge at 8 P.M., where it encountered the 37th Mississippi. In the darkness, the Mississippians misidentified Mower's men as Confederates, and when the Missourians started firing, the Southerners cried out "for God's sake, stop firing into your own men." Mower continued firing, and repulsed three separate bayonet charges from the stubborn Rebels. The major of the 11th Missouri described the ferocity of the combat, writing that "in several instances the enemy was received on the point of the bayonet and then shot off, and others were shot by officers, who placed their pistols in their very faces." After expending their ammunition, the Missourians disengaged, and darkness mercifully put an end to the killing.[29]

In his report of the battle, Price stated that the struggle "was waged with a severity which I have never seen sur-

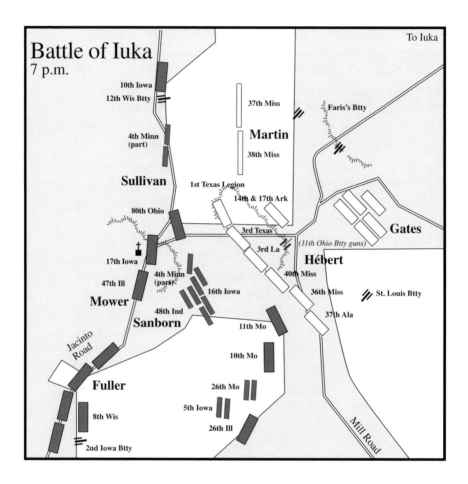

Battle of Iuka
7 p.m.

To Iuka

10th Iowa
12th Wis Btty

4th Minn
(part)

Sullivan

80th Ohio

17th Iowa

47th Ill

Mower

4th Minn
(part)

16th Iowa

48th Ind

Sanborn

11th Mo

10th Mo

26th Mo

5th Iowa

26th Ill

Fuller

8th Wis

2nd Iowa Btty

Jacinto
Road

37th Miss

Martin

38th Miss

1st Texas Legion

14th & 17th Ark

3rd Texas

3rd La

40th Miss

Faris's Btty

Gates

(11th Ohio Btty guns)

Hébert

36th Miss

37th Ala

St. Louis Btty

Mill Road

passed," and that it was "the hardest-fought fight which I have ever witnessed." Union General Hamilton agreed, stating "I never saw a hotter or more destructive engagement." After the combat finally stopped, Rosecrans began reorganizing the Army of the Mississippi to repel a continued attack in the morning. He deployed Stanley's division in place of Hamilton and sent a dispatch to Grant, from whom he had not received any communication in more than ten hours. Perplexed and frustrated by the recent turn of events, Rosecrans wrote, "the engagement lasted several hours. We have lost two or three pieces of artillery. Firing was very heavy. You must attack in the morning and *in force*. The ground is horrid, unknown to us, and no room for development. . . . Push into them until we can have time to do something." The note would not reach Grant's headquarters in Burnsville until 8:35 A.M. the next morning, and by that time, events had occurred that would render any such attack impossible.[30]

4

"O, THAT CORINTH COULD BE LEFT TO TAKE CARE OF ITSELF!"

At 8:35 A.M. Maj. Gen. Ulysses S. Grant received Brig. Gen. William S. Rosecrans's dispatch from the night before, informing him of the desperate struggle and urgently requesting his support. This was Grant's first notification that a battle had occurred at all, and he instantly sent a message to Maj. Gen. Edward O.C. Ord, ordering him "to attack as soon as possible." Grant emphasized the necessity of rapid movement, stressing that "Rosecrans had two hours' fighting last night. . . . and unless you can create a diversion in his favor he may find his hands full. Hurry your troops." Ord advanced, but upon his arrival in Iuka, he discovered only deserted Confederate defenses and a very embittered Rosecrans now occupying the town.[1]

Under the enveloping shroud of night, Maj. Gen. Sterling Price redeployed his forces. The remaining two brigades of Brig. Gen. Henry Little's division, now commanded by Brig.

Dabney Herndon Maury

Born in Virginia in 1822, Maury graduated from the University of Virginia in 1842 and then attended the U.S. Military Academy where he graduated thirty-seventh of fifty-nine in the class of 1846. Brevetted second lieutenant and assigned to the Regiment of Mounted Rifles, he fought in the Mexican War and was wounded in the arm at Cerro Gordo, and brevetted first lieutenant. Afterwards he returned to West Point to teach. He was stationed on the Texas frontier at the outbreak of Civil War and joined the Confederate army as a captain of cavalry in June 1861. He was promoted to colonel in February 1862, and then to chief of staff for Maj. Gen. Earl Van Dorn at Pea Ridge. He became a brigadier general in March 1862, and fought well while leading a division at the battle of Corinth in October 1862. He was promoted to major general in November 1862 and sent to Vicksburg in December and gave good service during the early defense of that post. Maury was named commander of the Department of East Tennessee in April 1863, and in May became commander of the District of the Gulf, headquartered at Mobile.

He dutifully defended the city with all his energy and limited resources, but in April 1865, overwhelmed by superior Federal forces, he was forced to evacuate. He surrendered the following month as part of Lt. Gen. Richard Taylor's command. After the war, Maury founded and taught at a boy's school in Fredericksburg, Virginia. In 1868, he organized the Southern Historical Society and served as executive chair until 1886. He served as U.S. minister to Columbia from 1885 to 1889, and upon his return to the United States, lived with his son in Peoria, Illinois, until his death in January 1900. Dabney Maury is best described as a fine Virginia gentlemen who served honorably as a productive soldier, writer, teacher, and civil servant.

Gen. Louis Hébert, were brought forward to the ridge to replace Hébert's depleted brigade. The brigades of colonels Elijah Gates and John D. Martin held the front line, while Brig. Gen. Martin Green's brigade was posted as a reserve. Brig. Gen. Dabney Maury's division marched southward from Ord's position northwest of Iuka to support a planned continuation of the attack at sunrise. The men slept on their weapons, so close to the enemy that Federal commands could be heard. "Here we passed one of the most thrilling nights of my existence," one of Price's Missourians recalled, "The heavy dew fell cold and cheerless,—not a soul was allowed to stir, as the breaking of a twig might cause a fire." In the darkness, a Southerner attempted to light his pipe and instead sparked an exchange of musketry through the trees, which one soldier remembered as being "illuminated with fitful flashes running along the ground for a mile or so to the right and left, like the lightning in a summer sky playing on the western horizon."[2]

While advancing, one Missouri company unintentionally stepped on a wounded Federal, who cried out, "Don't tread on me." The Confederates asked the man, "What regiment do you belong to?" The Northerner responded, "The Thirty-ninth Ohio." The Southerners continued their questioning, inquiring, "How many men does Rosecrans have?" to which the Ohioan, intending to misinform his adversaries, answered, "Near forty-five thousand." An Irish Rebel replied in kind, asserting without hesitation that "our sixty-five thousand are enough for them."[3]

As the Confederates reformed their ranks on the battlefield, a landscape of intense bloodshed and human suffering overwhelmed them. One Missourian described the horrific scene years later, recalling that the "moon was nearly full, and threw a strong light upon the pale and ghastly faces of the thickly strewn corpses. . . . The dead were so thick, that one could very readily have stepped about upon them. . . . the desperate nature of the struggle was unmistakable. The carnage around the battery was terrible." Nightmarish sights and sounds of agonizing death surrounded the six captured cannons of Lieutenant Sears's 11th Ohio Battery. The Missourian viewed the wreckage and continued, "one of the caissons was turned upside down. . . . and immediately behind was a pile of not less than fifteen men, who had been killed and wounded. . . . They were all Federals, and most of them artillery-men." The soldier in gray ended his account by emphasizing the savagery of the fight for Sears's guns: "strewn thickly around all were the bloody corpses of the dead, while the badly wounded lay weltering in gore. I have been on many battlefields, but never witnessed so small a space comprise as many dead as were lying around this battery."[4]

The tortured cries of the wounded echoed throughout the night, some begging for water, some praying to God, and still others pleading to be shot and "put out of their misery." Thomas Abbott of the 17th Arkansas ventured into the no man's land between the lines with a small party to search for a missing friend. He wrote later that "we found our comrade mortally wounded and tried to take him to the hospital, but could not get within forty yards of it, for the dead and wounded." The Confederate wounded were taken to Iuka, where every major building had been converted into a hospital. Across the lines, Federal surgeons performed amputations by candlelight, operating without any anesthetics, which only added to the acute cruelty of the engagement. Witnesses present in the Union field hospital pronounced it "a night of horrors."[5]

The most significant loss to the South was that of Brig. Gen. Henry Little, whose body was returned to Iuka following his death. During the night, a member of Little's staff, Capt. Frank von Phul, went to General Price's headquarters to ascertain his final wishes for the fallen general. The aid located the commander, noting that the "lines of sorrow were like furrows on his brow." Von Phul addressed the weary Price, "General, what shall I do with General Little's body?" Grieving deeply, Price could only respond, "My Little, my Little; I've lost my Little." After a brief pause, Von Phul repeated the question, only to receive the same reply. After a third and final request, Price answered somberly, "My Little is gone; I've lost my Little." Von Phul, realizing the futility of his efforts, left headquarters without instructions, writing later that Price "was almost crazed with grief, and I don't believe he knew what I was asking him."[6]

Von Phul met with Col. Thomas Snead, Price's Chief of Staff, who promised to speak to the general himself about the matter. At 10 o'clock Price reached a decision to bury Little as soon as possible. A small detail quickly dug a grave in a garden behind headquarters, and the coffin was lowered into the Mississippi soil by what Von Phul designated as "the saddest funeral train I ever witnessed in my life." The grief-stricken entourage held a short candlelight service, and then the Marylander was laid to rest. Von Phul remembered that "it was just midnight as the last spadefull of earth was placed upon the grave and patted into shape. Our candles still flickered in the darkness, sending out weird shadows. A plain piece of pine board was set at the head marked: General Henry Little."[7]

Following the impromptu funeral, Price retired for the night, leaving strict orders that he was not to be awakened until an hour before daylight. After midnight, General Hébert arrived at headquarters, warning Colonel Snead that his brigade "was so badly cut up" and his division so demoralized by the death of General Little that he worried about continuing the battle. Around 2 A.M. General Maury appeared, along with cavalry commanders Brig. Gen. Frank Armstrong and Col. Wirt Adams. Maury was convinced that if the Army of the West remained between Grant and Rosecrans its "total destruction seemed inevitable." The officers demanded to speak with Price, and when a courier from Maj. Gen. Earl Van Dorn rode up, Snead consented to wake up the commanding general.[8]

Maury presented his argument for an immediate withdrawal, but as he stated later, "the old man was hard to move." Maury perceived that since Price "had taken a personal part in the battle that evening; his Missourians had behaved beautifully under his own direction, the enemy had been so freely driven back, that he could think of nothing but the complete victory he would gain over Rosecrans in the morning." Price answered Maury's concerns with confident assurances of success, to the point that the division commander felt that Price

A *Harper's Weekly* sketch of Iuka, Mississippi, from the October 4, 1862 issue.

"seemed to take no account of Grant at all." The other officers delivered their appraisals of the situation, unanimously calling for a retreat. Maury persevered, declaring firmly that "as sure as we resume battle, placed as we are, we shall be beaten, and we shall lose every wagon. You can't procure another wagon train like this, not if you were to drain the State of Mississippi of all its teams." In a final statement, Maury asserted that "we have won the fight this evening. We decided on going back anyhow in the morning to Baldwin, and I don't see that anything that has happened since we published that decision should detain us here any longer."[9]

Faced with such opposition, Price relented and gave the order to evacuate Iuka as soon as possible. The wagons had already been loaded during the day, and were moving out along the Fulton Road by 3 A.M. The infantry soon followed, and by 8 A.M. the last of Price's men had left Iuka. The Confederates left behind the seriously wounded and a few stragglers in the town, along with the six captured cannon of Sears's battery. A shortage of horses compelled Price to leave his hard-won trophies behind, spiked with files driven through their touchholes, preventing any future use until repairs could be performed. The Rebels conducted the retreat at a breakneck pace, abandoning and burning any wagon that broke down along the way. "Old Pap," dressed in a colorful battle shirt that he called his "war-coat," oversaw the operation, motivating his men and threatening the drivers that "if one of you stops, I'll hang you, by G-d."[10]

The Federals heard the noises of the early morning movement as they waited apprehensively for the coming dawn. Rosecrans, a habitual night-owl, had remained awake all night uncertain if the sounds indicated that Price was retreating or merely repositioning his forces for another assault. Although "Old Rosy" reported that he was "profoundly disappointed" Grant had not attacked Price, he nonetheless decided to push forward with Brig. Gen. David Stanley's division at sunrise. As he gave his instructions to his commanders, he asked General Stanley in frustration, "where, in the name of God, is Grant?" At first light Federal skirmishers advanced toward the Confederate lines and encountered no resistance. The Army of the West had escaped.[11]

When Rosecrans demanded to know why he had been left unsupported on the previous day, Ord explained that neither he nor Grant had heard any sounds of fighting. A combination of wind, broken terrain, and heat had created a phenomenon known as an acoustic shadow, in which sound waves are distorted away from a particular area by intervening factors. Ord was only six miles away from the battlefield, and normally the thunder of artillery and the crash of thousands of muskets would have been clearly audible at his position. That afternoon, however, a strong south wind had blown through the trees, preventing the noise of battle from reaching Burnsville. Around 6 P.M., Ord received a report of thick smoke rising from Iuka, but without the corresponding clamor it was assumed that Price was merely burning his supplies in preparation to retreat. Rosecrans, remembering Maj. Gen. George McClellan's failure to support his flanking assault at the Battle of Rich Mountain, could find little solace in this justification.[12]

Rumors quickly began to spread that Grant, after receiving the wire proclaiming the war to be won at Antietam, started celebrating prematurely. One of Rosecrans's men grumbled that "General Grant was dead drunk and couldn't bring up his army. I was so mad when I first learned the facts that I could have shot Grant if I would have hung for it the next minute." There is no verification that Grant was intoxicated on the 19th, rather it appears that he was satisfied that Rosecrans could not reach Iuka before the morning of the 20th, and the consequences of an acoustic shadow and atrocious communications prohibited him from knowing otherwise. Another Ohioan wrote that "the impression is against General Ord for being too late. Bulldog bravery of the men in the ranks and darkness changed what would otherwise have been a defeat into a drawn battle."[13]

If Rosecrans was suspicious about his superior's failure to attack, Grant was equally disappointed to learn that the Fulton Road had been left uncovered, which allowed Price to slip out of Grant's trap. Although his ambitious snare had been thwarted, a personal inspection of the topography led him to revise his opinion and accept Rosecrans's judgment. He admitted in his report that "a partial examination of the country afterward convinced me, however, that troops moving in separate columns by the routes suggested could not support each other until they arrived near Iuka." An immediate pursuit of Price was mounted with cavalry and Hamilton's division, but it was called off after a sharp encounter with the Confederate rear guard. General Hamilton later explained the futility of the chase, writing that "a pursuit of a defeated enemy can amount to little in a country like that of Northern Mississippi, heavily wooded, and with narrow roads, when the enemy has time enough to get his artillery and trains in front of his infantry."[14]

Union soldiers were shocked when they saw the contested ridge, littered with debris from the previous day's engagement. One Federal noticed that near the wreckage of Sears's battery "twelve horses belonging to two caissons had become tangled together and piled up like a pyramid." He remarked that the image, along with "our dead heroes and those of the enemy lying thickly over the ground and the look of destruction and desolation that abounded in the vicinity, was the grandest and most awful spectacle of war that I viewed during a service of four and a half years." A member of the 15th Iowa, Sgt. Cyrus Boyd, visited the Confederate wounded in town. He recalled in horror that "some of them were deranged and looked horrible as they raved and rolled in their blood[.] Some had their legs and some their arms amputated." Boyd encountered one Texan that was wounded severely, and described the soldier as, "pluck to the core. . . . He took a large minnie ball from his vest pocket and showed me[.] The ball was flattened and he said he got that in his hip last spring at *Shiloh* from the '*Yanks*' and now he had another in him." The Texan resolutely informed Boyd that "he expected to be up again and as soon as he could he would be after us again. I said 'Bully for you old boy' and bid him good bye."[15]

The Battle of Iuka was a costly fight for both armies. The Union Army of the Mississippi lost 141 killed, 613 wounded, and 36 missing, for a total of 790 casualties in an engagement that did not last more than three hours. The 5th Iowa suffered the worst loss of any Federal regiment, reporting 37 killed, 179 wounded, and 1 man missing, which represented almost half of their strength. On the other side, Price acknowledged 85 killed, 410 wounded, and 157 missing, which was an incredibly light amount considering the strength of the position attacked and the vicious fire delivered by the Yankees. Union witnesses testified to burying 265 Confederates and capturing a large number of prisoners and wounded that were too weak to be evacuated. Rosecrans estimated the Confederate loss to be 1,438, and other Federal assessments are comparable. Incorporating this evidence, a conservative estimate puts Price's losses at the minimum of a 1,000, perhaps as high as 1,500. In stark contrast, Ord's detachment had only suffered one man wounded during the entire day.[16]

Iuka was an intense, but inconclusive, collision of armies. After the battle, Grant observed that "if it was the object of the enemy to make their way into Kentucky, they were defeated in that; if to hold their position until Van Dorn could come up on the southwest of Corinth and make a simultaneous attack, they were defeated in that." He concluded that "our only defeat was in not capturing the entire army or destroying it, as I had hoped to do." The battle was a strategic draw. Although both sides claimed victory, neither had actually won. Price had preserved his army despite being taken by surprise, and inflicted terrible damage on the Northerners, but he had suffered grievously as well. Grant had bloodied his opponent, but not subdued him. Only an accident of nature prevented the total destruction of the Army of the West, and only the sudden death of General Little saved Hamilton's division from total collapse. Control of northern Mississippi and West Tennessee was still unresolved. More blood would have to be shed to determine the outcome.[17]

Nine days after the fight, Sergeant Boyd revisited the battlefield. He recorded in his diary that "I have never seen before evidence of such a desperate contest on a small piece of ground." Federal burial parties had deposited the decomposing bodies in hastily dug trenches, prompting Boyd to write that he "saw many of the enemies dead lying around not more than half covered. The ground in many places was *white* as snow with *creeping worms.* The darkness of the forest and the terrible mortality made it one of the most *horrible* places I was ever in." The Iowan reflected on the gruesome scene and added, "the *silence* was oppressive. Not a sound could be heard except once in a while the chirp of some lonely bird in the deep forest. To think of our poor fellows left to sleep in that dark wood (But one must not think of such things)."[18]

The Confederates withdrew southward to Baldwyn, Mississippi, in a rapid but disordered retreat. One soldier in gray remembered that "we made a march of twenty-five miles that day. . . . oh, how my feet were blistered! They felt as if I had my shoes filled with hot embers." The exhausted Southerners, plagued by poor discipline, suffered from severe straggling and several acts of looting. After a few days of rest in Baldwyn, Price marched his remaining forces to Ripley to unite with Van Dorn's Vicksburg army on September 28. The Mississippian Van Dorn, ever eager to restore his martial reputation, began marching northward toward Corinth to challenge his old West Point classmate, William S. Rosecrans.[19]

After the Battle of Iuka, Grant transferred his headquarters to Jackson, Tennessee, leaving Rosecrans in command of Corinth. While preparing his defenses against an expected Confederate advance, Rosecrans wrote to Grant on September 23, "O, that Corinth could be left to take care of itself!" When he received notification of a long awaited and well deserved promotion to major general, Rosecrans was furious to discover that it dated from September 17, 1862, rather than from his earlier West Virginia campaign. Not content with merely fighting the Rebels, "Old Rosy" simultaneously battled the War Department. On September 26, Rosecrans fumed to General in Chief Henry Halleck that "a feeling of shame and indignation came over me as I wrote the acceptance. . . . I find myself promoted junior to men who have not rendered a tithe of the services nor had a tithe of the success." The newly promoted major general declared that "were it not a crisis for the country I would not trouble you to intercede in my behalf but would resign at once. As it is a crisis I beg you intercede for me, that some measure of justice may be done me." Halleck, realizing Rosecrans was too capable a commander to lose, conceded the contest. Shortly thereafter President Lincoln amended the commission.[20]

Grant recognized the impending danger posed by the united Confederate armies and wired to Halleck on October 1 that "my position is precarious, but hope to get out of it all right." In Corinth, Rosecrans issued two days' rations and distributed ammunition to his divisions. A soldier of the 7th Illinois remarked that "these orders . . . we are inclined to think, mean business." This same Federal noted apprehensively that "there is certainly a storm coming. God only knows how soon the terrible din will be heard; only knows how soon there will be a rattle of musketry and a clash of steel; when more blood will flow, more hearts will bleed, and more tears will fall." The storm clouds of war were marching toward Corinth, waiting to be unleashed with a fury that no one on either side could have imagined.[21]

5

"WE SHALL SLEEP IN CORINTH TO-NIGHT"

Maj. Gen. Earl Van Dorn, upon taking command of what he personally christened as the Army of West Tennessee, confronted the most daunting mission of his military career. On September 18, Maj. Gen. John C. Breckinridge's division had been detached from Van Dorn's authority to reinforce Gen. Braxton Bragg's endeavor to secure Kentucky. Breckinridge, a prominent Kentucky politician and former Vice President of the United States, felt no sorrow to leave Van Dorn, particularly after his miserable experience at Baton Rouge. This left the "Defender of Vicksburg" with a single seven thousand man division under Maj. Gen. Mansfield Lovell, who bore his own stigma for losing New Orleans to Admiral Farragut in April. Both Lovell and Van Dorn were fervently committed to removing the stain of defeat that had tainted their honor and defiled their names throughout the long summer of 1862.[1]

MANSFIELD LOVELL

Born in Washington, D.C. in 1822, Lovell's father was the first surgeon general of the United States Army Medical Department. Lovell graduated from the United States Military Academy in 1842, ninth out of a class of fifty-six. During the Mexican War, he served as a 2d lieutenant in the 4th U.S. Artillery and was seriously wounded in combat at Belen Gate. After recovering, he earned a brevet promotion to captain for gallantry at Chapultepec and later served on the staff of Brig. Gen. John A. Quitman. In 1854, he left the army to pursue business opportunities at an iron works in New Jersey, and in 1858 was appointed superintendent of street improvements in New York City, where he later served as deputy street commissioner. In 1861, along with his friend Gustavus W. Smith, Lovell traveled to Richmond and offered his services to the Confederacy. Commissioned as a brigadier general, Lovell was assigned to command the vital port of New Orleans, the largest and most important city in the South. Plagued by a severe lack of men and material, Lovell was forced to abandon the Crescent City in April 1862 after Union Adm. David Farragut's warships broke past the defenses of Forts Jackson and St. Philip. Unfairly held responsible for the New Orleans disaster, Lovell was subsequently transferred to command a division in Maj. Gen. Earl Van Dorn's Vicksburg garrison, which he led during Van Dorn's autumn 1862 expedition into Northern Mississippi. At the battle of Corinth, Lovell showed little aggression on the first day of battle and failed to commit his division to the disastrous final Confederate assault on the second. After serving as the army's rear guard during the retreat, Lovell was relieved from command and subjected to a court of inquiry for his actions at New Orleans. Although he was acquitted of all charges in July 1863, Lovell never again held a serious command during the war and was known disparagingly as "Lord Lovell," for his prideful manner and alcohol-related red nose. After surrendering to Federal troops in 1865, Lovell attempted to restore his fortunes by purchasing a rice plantation in Georgia, but his crops were destroyed by a tidal wave. Lovell then returned to New York City, where he lived out the rest of his life as a civil engineer and surveyor. He died there in 1884 and is buried in Woodlawn Cemetery.

On September 28, Maj. Gen. Sterling Price had arrived in Ripley with the remaining men of the Army of the West, worn down by a grueling march through a severe thunderstorm. Brig. Gen. Dabney Maury's division contained 3,866 effective soldiers, while Brig. Gen. Louis Hébert managed to retain 6,602 survivors from Iuka. In all, "Old Pap" contributed 14,363 veterans of all arms to the operation, which when combined with Lovell's division and the cavalry, gave Earl Van Dorn a total of 22,000 men to drive back the Northerners and liberate West Tennessee.[2]

Facing him were approximately 42,000 Federals, dispersed at various garrisons throughout the area. Van Dorn originally intended to draw the Union forces out of the breastworks and fight in the open on favorable ground, emulating the tactics that Stonewall Jackson had used so brilliantly in the Shenandoah Valley. On September 3, Van Dorn had written to Price that "if Rosecrans remains at Corinth we had better join forces west of him and maneuver him out of that strong place, and at the same time prevent Grant and Sherman from joining him. We should try to shake them loose from all points in West Tennessee; then march to join Bragg, if necessary." On September 24, while Price was in Baldwyn recovering from his Iuka escape, Van Dorn expressed a surprising word of caution to Price, "if it becomes necessary to wait it will not be unfortunate, as we are holding a large force in check; later we will defeat them, free West Tennessee and penetrate Kentucky or cross the Ohio. I do not think it necessary to act hurriedly." This was a rare display of restraint from the ever zealous Van Dorn, who concluded his dispatch speculating that, "on the contrary, a little delay, attacking, as it were, *en echelon* from Maryland to West Tennessee and Arkansas, seems to me advisable."[3]

On September 25, Bragg wired Van Dorn and urged him to march northward at once. Bragg was convinced that Union defenses in Tennessee were drastically weakened and exhorted

Van Dorn to "sweep them off and push up to the Ohio. . . . All depends on rapid movements. Trusting to your energy and zeal we shall confidently expect a diversion in our favor against the overwhelming forces now concentrating against us." Mysteriously, Van Dorn reported that he did not receive the message until November. On the same day that Bragg transmitted his appeal to Van Dorn, he also wrote privately to President Davis and complained that "there has been a want of cordial co-operation on the part of Genl Van Dorn since his department was merged into mine. The general is most true to our cause and gallant to a fault, but he is self willed, rather weak minded & totally deficient in organization and system." Bragg contended that Van Dorn "never knows the state of his command and wields it in only in fragments."[4]

Van Dorn, despite his communication difficulties, could feel the pressure mounting upon him for a swift and decisive counterstroke. Using intelligence gathered by a Confederate spy in Corinth, Van Dorn detected vulnerability in the Federal positions and determined to act immediately. Grant had concentrated his forces in three heavily defended garrisons, all connected by rail lines, enabling reinforcements to arrive quickly if any one of the three were threatened. Sherman held the left flank at Memphis with around six thousand Union soldiers, Gen. Stephen Hurlbut protected Grant's center at Bolivar, Tennessee, with eight thousand, Rosecrans was posted on the right of the line with fifteen thousand men at Corinth, and another ten thousand Federals maintained outlying stations and guarded bridges. If Van Dorn could surprise one of the strongholds before it could be reinforced, he would have a decided advantage in strength.[5]

Van Dorn observed that out of all possible targets, "Corinth is the strongest but most salient point." A strike at Memphis would be futile without effective naval support, and defensive works on both banks of the Hatchie River shielded Bolivar, denying any possibility of a sudden attack. An advance directly

The Tishomingo Hotel and railroad tracks in Corinth circa 1862.
Francis Miller's Photographic History of the Civil War.

into Tennessee would leave sizable Union detachments behind the Confederate army, threatening to cut the Southerners off or march southward to a lightly defended Vicksburg. But a daring direct assault upon Corinth could recapture the strategic rail junction and unhinge the entire Federal defensive front. Assessing the situation, Van Dorn concluded that the "taking of Corinth was a condition precedent to the accomplishment of anything of importance in West Tennessee."[6]

The conquest of Corinth would return Confederate control over the vital rail juncture and deny the Federals a critical

supply base. Six key roads intersected at Corinth, from which Van Dorn could continue to invade northward, opening the way to Kentucky. A successful drive into West Tennessee would also save Vicksburg and Port Hudson from a feared Union offensive along the Mississippi River. From his previous service on the river that summer, Van Dorn had realized that "a combined land and naval attack was necessary" to capture Vicksburg, and that "the enemy was exerting extraordinary energy to be prepared for such result." The only way to permanently secure the tenuous twin fortresses that held the southern Confederacy together was to deny Grant the foothold necessary to concentrate his forces and prepare his onslaught. Speed was imperative, as reports indicated that Corinth "was being strengthened daily under that astute soldier General Rosecrans."[7]

When Van Dorn detailed his audacious plan to General Price on the 28th, the Missourian admitted that Corinth "warranted more than the usual hazard of battle," but recommended waiting for the return of thousands of exchanged prisoners surrendered to Grant at Fort Donelson, which would postpone any forward movement for weeks. Van Dorn emphatically rejected the proposal, as neither he nor his superiors could wait any longer. At Pea Ridge, Price had received abundant praise for his conspicuous role in the fighting, while Van Dorn had received nothing more than the blame for the failed venture. Independently, Price had garnered more glory at Iuka on the 19th, only a few days before he again fell under Van Dorn's command. Now finally in control of the combined Confederate army in northern Mississippi, Van Dorn would assault Corinth directly and force Rosecrans's men to run, just as the Union soldiers had done the previous week. Price, with the memories of the bitter struggle still fresh in his mind, well understood the serious risks of the undertaking. After his suggestion of delay was refused, Van Dorn remarked, "you seem despondent, General Price." The Missourian responded sharply, "No! You quite mistake me. I have only given you the facts within my knowledge and the counseling of my judgment. When you reach Corinth you shall find that no portion of the army shall exceed mine either in courage, in conduct, or in achievement."[8]

As Price reluctantly accepted his assignment, the general received the discouraging notification that his faithful chief of staff, Maj. Thomas Snead, had resigned in protest rather than once again participate in a Van Dorn directed campaign. In his letter of resignation, Snead declared bluntly that "I cannot serve under Van Dorn. I hope that you will not ask me to do it. The sooner that you escape from him (but that is now impossible) the better." Snead feared that "General Damn-born," as Van Dorn was derisively known to the ranks, would lead Price and his men into another fruitless and disastrous failure. He detailed his concerns, but warned "I hope that my forebodings may prove false, but it seems to me that they are based on a firm foundation." Price reacted with empathy and acknowledged that "every Missourian here is impressed with feelings corresponding to yours," but the old politician contended that the "military position we at present occupy . . . with an engagement where the odds are heavy against us imminently impending, calls imperatively for a sacrifice on my part and that of my army of all that we feel to be due us." Pacified by Price's appeal to remain, Snead grudgingly withdrew his resignation.[9]

On September 29, the day the recently created Army of West Tennessee marched out of Ripley, an order arrived from Confederate Secretary of War George Wythe Randolph, directing Van Dorn to "assume forthwith the command of all troops left in Mississippi, including General Price's column. Concentrate them without loss of time; . . . make proper disposition for the defense of the Mississippi River, and also for an advance into Tennessee." Richmond's demand for action excited Van Dorn's cavalier blood and hardened his resolve to assault Corinth as soon as possible. There could be no hope of maneuvering or turning back now. If the daring gamble succeeded, the Federals would be driven all the way back to where Grant had started his first offensive in February.[10]

Van Dorn planned to advance his army thirty miles northward to Metamora, Tennessee, to deceive the Federals into believing that he intended to strike Bolivar. From there the Confederate force would turn eastward, cross the Hatchie and Tuscumbia Rivers, march ten miles to Chewalla, and then drive hell for leather the nine remaining miles to Corinth. Van Dorn would sweep down from the northwest, cut Rosecrans off from reinforcement, and hit the least prepared segment of the Union fortifications. Severe drought still plagued northern

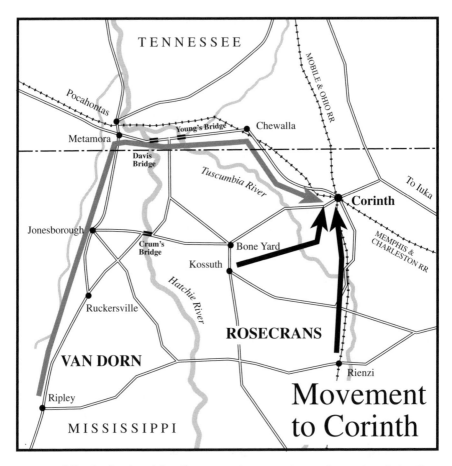

Movement to Corinth

Mississippi, with afternoon temperatures hovering into the nineties. After crossing the two rivers, the Army of West Tennessee would have no further source of water unless it could seize control of the wells at Corinth. Armed with an intricately detailed map of the surrounding area that was captured at Iuka, Van Dorn returned to a region he knew quite well. Incredibly, the Army of West Tennessee would now attack the exact same earthworks many of them had constructed during the siege of Corinth in April.[11]

Van Dorn's delicate timetable for the march was ruined almost instantly. Union cavalry harried the head of the

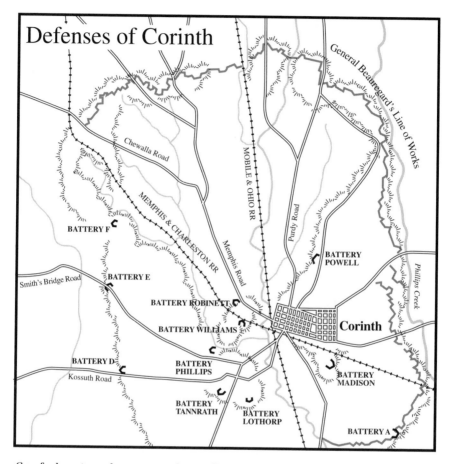

Defenses of Corinth

Confederate advance and set fire to bridges on both the Hatchie and Tuscumbia Rivers, which cost several precious hours to rebuild. The Federal horsemen lost no time in informing their superiors of the Confederate movement, which denied Van Dorn any chance of surprise. While waiting for repairs, Maj. Gen. Mansfield Lovell informed his brigade commanders of their mission. Brig. Gen. Albert Rust pronounced the assault to be "impossible" and described the entire operation "as madness," to which Lovell countered that if the attack did "not succeed we had better lay down our arms and go home." As the long gray columns turned south, the men in ranks realized with dread that their final objective was Corinth. One Louisianan recalled that "the men remembered the fortifications around this intrenched position, strengthened under the energetic labors of the enemy, and protected by heavy abattis of felled timber, and their hearts misgave then as to the final result when it was known where they were going into battle."[12]

Inside fortress Corinth, Rosecrans worked feverishly to improve his defenses to meet the threat presented by the man he referred to as "Buck Van Dorn." Corinth was defended by three distinct defensive lines from the northwest, including the old earthworks Beauregard had created during the siege. After penetrating the Beauregard Line, the Confederates would have to break through a second series of works in the Halleck Line and then breach the innermost fortifications before reaching the town. The final line was the strongest, containing seven well placed batteries: Robinett, Williams, Phillips, Tanrath, Lothrop, Madison, and Powell, each bristling with artillery. "Old Rosy" initially held Corinth with two divisions commanded by brigadier generals Thomas J. McKean and Thomas A. Davies, but when reports arrived of a large Confederate offensive, he ordered brigadier generals David Stanley and Charles Hamilton's divisions to redeploy inside the town. This augmentation increased the Federal garrison to 22,018 men, a force nearly equal to Van Dorn's army.[13]

Rosecrans, uncertain of his enemy's intentions, was prepared to either fight from his earthworks or march out and assault the Confederate flank if they bypassed Corinth. The Union general later remarked, "I knew that the enemy intended a strong movement, and I thought they must have the impression that our defensive works at Corinth would be pretty formidable. I doubted if they would venture to bring their force against our command behind defensive works." Nonetheless, during the night of October 2, Rosecrans ordered his men into position to resist a Confederate assault. McKean's division deployed along the Beauregard line directly to the west of

Corinth, astride the Chewalla Road and Memphis and Charleston tracks. Davies's division formed on their right, with Hamilton's division protecting the flank. Rosecrans remained at his headquarters in town, along with Stanley's division, which was held in reserve.[14]

By nightfall on October 2, the Army of West Tennessee had reached Chewalla, just nine miles short of the ultimate goal. At 4 A.M. on the 3rd, Van Dorn set his men in motion at a furious pace, hoping to capture Corinth in a single day's fight. The last few miles were spent skirmishing with a Federal infantry brigade under Col. John Oliver, from whom the Southerners captured one cannon. When the Northerners fell back to the earthworks in the Beauregard Line, Van Dorn deployed his brigades opposite the Federals, placing Lovell's division on the right and Price's old command to the left. Gen. Dabney Maury's men held the Confederate center, and Gen. Louis Hébert's division extended the line to the right. Van Dorn's tactical plan was to strike first with Lovell's men, provoking Rosecrans to draw upon his right for support, and then hammer the reduced Union flank with Price's determined veterans. As the Rebels formed their ranks, a Missourian joked to his friends that "we are in for some fun to-day." In response, one of his comrades proclaimed optimistically that "we will sleep in Corinth to-night." Shortly the before the long gray tide advanced, three small earthquake tremors convulsed the earth, which the soldiers interpreted as a grim forecast of defeat. At 10 A.M., Lovell's three brigades began to move forward.[15]

Opposing Lovell's men was the Union brigades of Colonel Oliver and Brig. Gen. John McArthur, posted on a steep wooded hill alongside the Memphis and Charleston tracks. McArthur, a hard-fighting and hard-drinking immigrant from Scotland, was ordered by Rosecrans to take command of both brigades and delay the Confederate advance. But as Rosecrans later observed, "McArthur's Scotch blood rose," and the Union general resolved to fight the Rebels for every inch of ground.

JOHN MCARTHUR

Born in Erskine, Scotland in 1826, McArthur attended a parish school and was trained in the art of blacksmithing by his father. In 1849, he immigrated to the United States and worked for a boiler-maker in Chicago before becoming a partner in the Excelsior Iron Works, which he gained full ownership of in 1858. During the late 1850s, McArthur was active in the local militia and rose to the rank of captain in the "Chicago Highland Guards," a company predominantly composed of Scottish immigrants. In May 1861, McArthur was appointed colonel of a ninety-day regiment, the 12th Illinois Infantry, which reenlisted for the war at the end of their term. Stationed at Cairo, Illinois, McArthur was promoted to command of a brigade in Ulysses S. Grant's District of Cairo in late 1861, and accompanied Grant in his successful expeditions against Forts Henry and Donelson in early 1862. In March 1862, he was promoted to brigadier general for his "meritorious service" at Fort Donelson, and that April at Shiloh, McArthur assumed command of the division when its commander, Gen. W.H. Wallace, was mortally wounded. In September, McArthur joined Grant's advance against Iuka, Mississippi, as part of Gen. Edward Ord's wing, and in October he served with distinction commanding a division under William S. Rosecrans at the battle of Corinth. After Corinth, McArthur was officially

When the Confederates approached the hill, McArthur's men unleashed a devastating fire that staggered the attackers. One of Lovell's brigade commanders, Brig. Gen. Albert Rust, recalled the intense carnage of the scene: "men were subjected to a test that it is rarely the lot of soldiers to undergo. . . . For a moment it appeared the entire line would be swept away. . . . In a few seconds I here lost over 100 men and officers."[16]

Unknown to McArthur, a mile-long breach existed between his right flank and Davies's division, which was itself stretched thin opposite Price's forces. As Rust's men overlapped the Union left flank, Brig. Gen. John C. Moore's brigade of Maury's division slammed through the hole, and McArthur's outnum-

given command of the 6th Division, XVII Corps, which he led effectively throughout the Vicksburg campaign. After the surrender of the city, McArthur was appointed to command the occupation, and along with other accomplished officers, he received a gold medal for his actions with the Army of the Tennessee. During this time, U.S. Grant attempted to have McArthur promoted to major general for his service, but without political support in Washington, the measure failed. In August 1864, Gen. William T. Sherman gave McArthur command of a district in Northern Georgia protecting his vital supply lines, and after the fall of Atlanta, McArthur was transferred to command of the 1st Division, XVI Corps, operating against Confederate Gen. Sterling Price's raid into Missouri. In December 1864, the XVI Corps returned east to reinforce Nashville against Confederate Gen. John Bell Hood's desperate invasion of Tennessee, and during the battle of Nashville, McArthur led an attack that devastated the Confederate left flank. For this success, McArthur was brevetted major general, and he subsequently served under Gen. Edward Canby during the capture of Mobile, Alabama. During the war, McArthur had compiled a combat record that few on either side could equal, and he rightly earned a reputation as one of the hardest fighting generals in the Union Army. At the end of the war, McArthur returned to his ironworks in Chicago, which unfortunately failed. In 1871, while serving as commissioner of public works, the Great Chicago fire erupted, and during his term as postmaster of the city he was forced to personally repay $70,000 of Federal funds lost in a bank failure. Despite his postwar business problems, McArthur was held in high regard and served notably in the Presbyterian Church, the St. Andrew's Society, the Grand Army of the Republic, and the Loyal Legion. John McArthur died in 1906 and is buried in Rosehill Cemetery in Chicago.

bered troops broke for the rear. The 9th Arkansas, known as the "Preachers regiment" because forty-two ministers had enlisted in its ranks, stormed up the hill, followed by Brig. Gen. John Bowen's brigade of Lovell's division. The Southerners rushed forward, determined to deliver the wrath of God to the hated invader. One of Bowen's men noted that "an exhilarating frenzy seemed to take possession of every man," and that "all seemed infused with the sublime horror of the occasion, and to a man we rushed over that embankment, up the hill to the very mouth of the cannon, killing the gunners at the guns and silencing the battery." The Confederates seized a 20 lbs. Parrott rifle, which had been named the "Lady Richardson" by its crew. With the Northerners on the run, Lovell discovered the redoubts of the Halleck Line to his front, and astoundingly, halted his attack. Despite repeated protests from his brigade commanders to continue the assault before the Federals could rally, Lovell refused to advance further for the rest of the day, even though little stood between his men and Corinth. Van Dorn, at the time directing Price's divisions, was out of contact with Lovell and unable to order him to press forward. Lovell's squandered opportunity cost Van Dorn his best chance for victory. Rosecrans would make Van Dorn pay dearly for that mistake.[17]

Shortly after Lovell's division stepped off, Van Dorn directed Price to unleash his onslaught on the Confederate left. "Old Pap," clad in his colorful "war coat," immediately ordered his men to charge. Davies's Federals, flanked on their left by Moore's Confederate brigade, were quickly overwhelmed and lost two cannons to the Rebels before escaping. A Missourian remarked that "away our brave fellows went, running helter skelter, over, under and through the trees, yelling like so many devils incarnate, and of course they drove the enemy from their breastworks and turned their guns upon them to assist them in their precipitate retreat." After clearing the Beauregard Line and chasing the Yankees for almost half a mile, Price was forced to interrupt his assault at 1:30 P.M. to allow his exhausted men to recover from their exertions. The limited water supplies and soaring temperature had drained the energy of his two divisions, and men on both sides were collapsing from heat exhaustion and dehydration. After a short rest, at 2:30 P.M. Price ordered his men to continue moving forward.[18]

During the respite, the Federals under Davies and McArthur reformed their ranks and summoned reinforcements. One of McArthur's men in the 7th Illinois described the arduous weather as "the heat is intense; no water; the men are famishing; some of the Seventh fall in their tracks, fainting and exhausted under the scorching sun." Amazingly, the aggressive

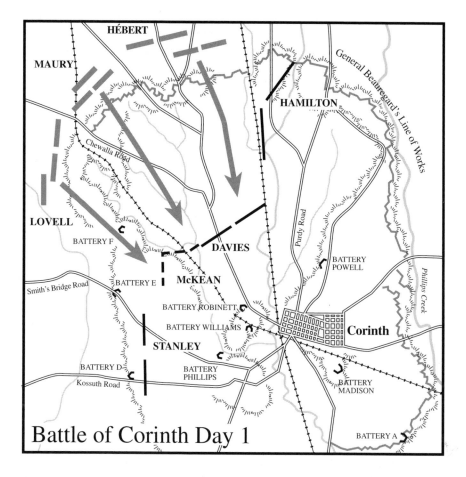

Battle of Corinth Day 1

Scotsman boldly counterattacked the Confederates, and briefly pushed back Moore's hard-charging veterans. Moore, reinforced by his reserves and two regiments from Cabell's brigade, renewed his assault and punched through McArthur's tired men, then slammed into Col. Marcellus Crocker's Iowa Brigade. One of Crocker's men, Cyrus Boyd, wrote in his diary that the Confederates had "three distinct lines one behind the other and all advancing in the most deliberate manner at *bayonets fixed*. We could hear the commands of the Rebel Officers distinctly." As the Confederates approached their lines, Boyd recalled that the Iowans "got upon one knee and had guns all cocked and ready when the front Regiments of the enemy took deliberate aim at us and the whole line fired into us and we heard the Rebel shout and *yell*." Crocker's men fought stubbornly but were slowly driven back. Boyd concluded his account, recording that "the battle raged fiercely for a time and men fell in great numbers. . . . the whole Regiment began to fall back not having even time to pick up the wounded but left them to their *fate*." Completely worn out, Moore's men could fight no further and contented themselves by enjoying the spoils of war captured from abandoned Federal camps.[19]

While generals McArthur and Moore dueled one another, on the Union right General Davies redeployed his remaining men in an open field in front of a small white house, 725 yards from the final defensive line. Reinforced by Col. Joseph Mower's brigade of Stanley's division, Davies created a daunting obstacle to impede the continued Confederate advance. At 3:30 P.M. Price's men emerged from the timber and were immediately raked by salvos of double canister from the eleven remaining Federal cannon. After pouring more than 1,500 rounds into the Rebels, the artillery exhausted their ammunition, forcing them to withdraw to the inner fortifications. In his report of the battle, Davies observed that the retreating cannoneers looked "more like coal-heavers than soldiers, with perspiration streaming down their faces blackened with gunpowder, and the wounded horses leaving a stream of blood in the road."[20]

Sensing their opportunity, Price's men rose up and rushed savagely into the Yankees. The two sides blasted away at one another for what seemed like an eternity in a close range, brutal struggle for survival. One Missourian remarked later that "the fighting became dogged. All the animal in man was aroused. No one seemed to think of death; the ruling impulse was to destroy." The heat was so intense that rounds exploded as they were being rammed down the rifles and hands were blistered from coming into contact with the scorching iron barrels. The same Missourian illustrated the fury he found himself in, writing that "if a soldier's ammunition became exhausted, he replenished his box from that of the dead. If his gun became fouled or overheated, he gathered another from a disabled comrade and fought on till crumpled up by an enemy bullet. . . . The air was full of whizzing missiles of death."[21]

Late in the afternoon, Price contributed the brigades of Col. Elijah Gates and Brig. Gen. C.W. Phifer to the assault, finally breaking Davies's thin blue line of soldiers. As Phifer's men pressed toward the Federals, a Texan recalled that "in a moment the whole air seemed to be literally filled with grape shot and shell. Our ranks were fearfully thinned, the boys falling in every direction. In our company every commission officer, save 3 Lieutenants was wounded and many of the soldiers killed." In Mower's brigade, the 8th Wisconsin had been unwisely issued whiskey by their quartermaster before entering the fight. When the Rebel tide burst upon them, the regiment collapsed and dashed unsteadily for the rear, accompanied by their remarkable mascot, a live bald eagle named "Old Abe." During the battle, an observer noted that "the eagle was delirious in the delight of the strange wild storm, his wings were beating and he gave screams of frantic joy." A Confederate bullet severed the rope that bound the frenzied bird to his perch, and "Old Abe" soared above the blue ranks, targeted by several southern muskets. The eagle's handler could do nothing more than chase after the wayward mascot, dodging bullets while he attempted to recover the terrified bird. Eventually, as one Northerner reported, the eagle "saw the gleam of the colors below and with magnificent swoop returned to his perch beside the Union flag." With their beloved mascot saved, the inebriated 8th stumbled back into Corinth.[22]

All throughout the long afternoon, Rosecrans tried unsuccessfully to mount a counterattack with Hamilton's unengaged division, which was posted on the Union far right and had fall-

The Battle of Corinth, Mississippi by Currier & Ives. *Library of Congress.*

en back when the Beauregard Line was lost. Around 3:00 P.M., Rosecrans dispatched his chief of staff, Col. Arthur Ducat, with written instructions for Hamilton to drive deep into Van Dorn's exposed left flank. But Hamilton was unnerved by an error in the order's wording that directed him to advance on Davies left flank, when it should have indicated the right flank. Amazingly, Hamilton refused to proceed, despite Ducat's passionate objections. Furious at his subordinate's indecision, Rosecrans immediately sent revised orders clarifying his intentions. When two messengers were killed by Rebel skirmishers before reaching the hesitant division commander, "Old Rosy," decided to resend Ducat. Ducat begged Rosecrans to reconsider, exclaiming, "I have four children." Rosecrans responded abruptly, "you knew that when you entered the service." Ducat arrived safely, but by the time Hamilton finally began his attack, daylight was fading quickly. One of his two brigades got lost and never fired a shot in anger, and the other only managed to capture a few prisoners before darkness ended the assault. Frustrated in his counterstrike, Rosecrans later grumbled that Hamilton's bungling did nothing more than give the "enemy a terrific scare."[23]

By dusk the Confederate Army of West Tennessee was within six hundred yards of Corinth, exhausted but triumphant. Van Dorn, eager to make the final effort, wanted his men to press on through the last Federal line before Corinth, in a night assault if necessary. Price, with his ranks confused, his men worn out and bloodied, and his ammunition depleted, persuaded the impetuous Mississippian to wait until morning. Reluctantly, Van Dorn ordered the final attack to commence at dawn. In his report, Van Dorn wrote with pride that his men had endured "a ten miles' march over a parched country, on dusty roads, without water, getting into line of battle in forests with undergrowth, and the more than equal activity and determined courage displayed by the enemy, commanded by one of the ablest generals of the United States Army." On October 3, Van Dorn had come tantalizingly close to achieving his long sought after victory and redemption. On October 4, he would risk his entire army in a desperate gamble to win both.[24]

6
"War to the Knife"

As darkness descended over the battlefield, General Rosecrans reorganized his defenses. Under the glow of a brilliant full moon, he deployed Brig. Gen. Thomas J. McKean's division to the earthworks on the left, anchored between the guns of Batteries Tanrath and Phillips. To McKean's right, Brig. Gen. David Stanley's division centered on Battery Robinette, followed by Brig. Gen. Thomas A. Davies's three shot-up brigades, which extended the line to Battery Powell. From there Hamilton protected the right flank, holding one brigade in reserve. Before moving into position, General Davies warned Rosecrans not to rely on his depleted division. All three brigade commanders of Davies's division had been wounded, and the men were exhausted from the severe heat and bitter fighting. Initially, Rosecrans permitted the division to withdraw as a reserve into Corinth, but a personal inspection of the lines convinced "Old Rosy" that every man available was needed to hold back the inevitable Confederate assault.

Rosecrans promptly countermanded the order, forcing Davies's weary men to reform and march back to their original starting point, an unfinished section of the line near Battery Powell. Davies's costly redeployment pressed the limits of his soldiers' endurance, denying them any opportunity for sleep.[1]

At 11:30 P.M. Rosecrans penned a note to Grant, confidently writing, "if they fight us tomorrow I think we shall whip them. If they go to attack you we shall advance upon them." That night, Grant ordered Brig. Gen. James B. McPherson to take five regiments from Bethel, Tennessee, southward twenty-seven miles to reinforce Corinth. Grant also wired Maj. Gen. Stephen Hurlbut to march five thousand men down from Bolivar, Tennessee, to Davis Bridge and strike the Confederate rear. Rebel horsemen wrecked the railroad tracks and cut the telegraph wires north of Corinth so that all communications between Grant and Rosecrans had to be conveyed on horse-back to and from the nearest working station at Bethel. The long ride delayed any message sent by either commander from arriving for seven to eight hours. After dispatching his letter to Grant, Rosecrans journeyed to his right flank, where he furiously berated his bumbling division commander, Brig. Gen. Charles Hamilton. Still fuming over the botched flank attack, "Old Rosy" vented his dissatisfaction with characteristic intensity. Finally satisfied with the defensive arrangements, a fatigued Rosecrans laid down to sleep at 4 A.M.[2]

At 4:30 Rosecrans was violently awoken by a massive artillery bombardment. Van Dorn's strategy for the second day was a complete reversal of his original tactical design: on the Confederate left, Hébert's division would initiate the attack at sunrise, followed en echelon by Maury's division in the center, and then Lovell's division would complete the assault on the right. The Confederates, camped among the dead and wounded from the first day's fighting, anxiously waited throughout the night to meet their destiny at dawn. The soldiers in gray listened intently to the noise of Federal movements, hoping against hope that Rosecrans was retreating. Brig. Gen. Martin Green, who recognized the ominous sounds of falling timber, knew better. He bitterly realized that the Northerners were instead working feverishly to improve their entrenchments in order to butcher his men when the sun rose.[3]

Hébert's men were to confront the six heavy cannon of Battery Powell, while down the line Maury's division faced the three twenty pound Parrott rifles of Battery Robinette and the five thirty pound Parrotts in Battery Williams. On the right, Lovell's men would hit the equally formidable Battery Phillips. The walls of each Battery were around seven feet high and fronted by a five-to-ten foot deep ditch. All except Battery Powell were protected by an abatis of felled trees four hundred yards in front of each fort. Van Dorn would attempt to carry well established fortifications by a traditional direct assault, a feat that no one had accomplished thus far in the war. To have any chance of success, the attack would have to be carefully coordinated and launched at first light, overwhelming the Union troops before sunlight exposed the attackers. The Confederate soldiers were well aware the dangers that awaited them, and one Southerner recalled the uneasy rest of the Army of West Tennessee: "it was a most anxious night, and no doubt one must feel under such circumstances somewhat like the condemned 'emigrant,' in his Paris prison during the Reign of Terror, on the night before he is to be embraced by Madame La Guillotine."[4]

October 4 did not begin well for Earl Van Dorn. In the darkness, his cannoneers overshot their targets, accomplishing little other than arousing the Federals from their slumber. As the sun slowly began to rise, Union gunners in the well-placed Batteries returned fire on the silhouetted Southerners and quickly silenced the Confederate cannonade. In the early morning confusion, Union skirmishers rushed upon startled Confederate artillerymen and captured one field piece. As dawn broke, Rosecrans braced for an assault—but none came.[5]

Stunned by the silence, Van Dorn waited apprehensively for Hébert to move forward, and as the minutes went by, he frantically sent three separate members of his staff to search for the overdue Creole. Hébert did not appear until 7:00 A.M., when he reported to Van Dorn that he was too ill to lead the attack. Curiously, he had kept his physical condition to himself when Van Dorn gave him his instructions the night before. Hébert's timing could not have been worse. Speculation later claimed that Hébert simply could not bring himself to lead a charge that he considered hopeless, while others would allege that Hébert was secretly addicted to narcotics. Whether sick, stoned, or spineless, Hébert's inaction had fatally delayed Van Dorn's climatic onslaught, but the Mississippian had come too far to turn back now. Command of the division was passed to Gen. Martin Green, who had absolutely no idea of what Van Dorn's battle plan entailed.[6]

The men of Hébert's division had endured hard times since losing their beloved commander, Brig. Gen. Henry Little, at Iuka. Col. W.B. Colbert now led Hébert's old brigade, while Col. W.H. Moore assumed command of Green's brigade. Col. John D. Martin had been fatally wounded while leading his brigade in the opening assault on the previous day, and was replaced by Colonel Robert McLain. Three of the division's four brigade commanders had no real experience leading a unit of that size into battle, and their first major test would come against a well-entrenched enemy in a well-prepared position. Once informed of his mission, Green arranged the men as best he could on such short notice. On the right of the division, Gates and Moore would aim straight for Battery Powell. On the left, Colbert and McLain would move out and then pivot ninety degrees to the right, swinging down on Hamilton's division. At 10:00 A.M., after more than three hours of delay in the growing heat, Green's veterans unfurled their battle flags and began advancing slowly toward Corinth.[7]

Directly in the path of Gates and Moore's brigades lay Davies's weakened division, which was unintentionally placed in the most vulnerable portion of Rosecrans's entire defensive line, despite Davies's protests the night before. From Battery Powell to the tracks of the Mobile and Ohio Railroad no earthworks had been constructed, and Davies's drained men had neither the time nor the energy to prepare any before Green's assault. As the Confederates burst forth from out of the trees 350 yards in front of the fort, they immediately encountered what one survivor described "a perfect tornado of grape and canister." One Missourian, Sgt. James Payne, described the initial shock of the moment as "then burst the storm. Every red-mouthed cannon from the frowning brow of Robinette on the right, to the most distant lunette on the left, belched forth their destructive fire." Undaunted, the Rebels closed ranks and swiftly advanced to within rifle range. At that instant, the Federal infantry unleashed a devastating volley directly into the faces of the surging gray tide. Payne recalled that "a sheet of flame leaped out from fronting rifle pits and showers of iron and leaden hail smote the onrushing men from Missouri with terrible and deadly effect. . . . Bending their necks as do men when protecting themselves from storm-driven hailstones, they pressed rapidly ahead." It was, as one witness noted, an atmosphere "in which a single glance comprehended all that in battle is sublime, grand, and terrible."[8]

The Federal gunners in Battery Powell worked desperately, pouring double canister into the charging ranks as fast as possible. Sergeant Payne, pressing forward in W.H. Moore's brigade, recorded that "every instant death smote. It came in a hundred shapes, every shape a separate horror. Here a shell, short fused, exploding in the thinning ranks, would rend and leave its victims and spatter their comrades with brains, flesh, and blood." The Southerners emptied their muskets at point blank range and crashed into the worn out Yankees, shattering the thin blue line. General Davies wrote angrily in his report that one man "fired his piece in the air, ducked his head, and ran to the rear. . . . I only regret that I was not near enough to the cowards to have shot them down, as I had shot at two the day before on leaving the line under similar circumstances." As an incredulous Rosecrans watched helplessly, Davies's entire division collapsed.[9]

Gates's victorious men stormed into Battery Powell, driving the Northerners out in bitter hand-to-hand fighting. But Federal artillery on their flanks began pounding the exposed brigade, catching the Missourians in a deadly crossfire. James Payne remembered vividly that "men's heads were blown to atoms. Fragments of human flesh still quivering with life would slap other men in the face, or fall to earth to be trampled underfoot. Men went down in hundreds." Gates's bloodied brigade had cracked the Union center, but lacked the strength to destroy it. The worn-out Confederates looked to the rear for desperately needed reinforcements—and none came.[10]

On the Confederate left, Colbert's and McLain's brigades charged straight into a wall of fire from Hamilton's fresh division. Supporting Hamilton were the six repaired cannons of the 11th Ohio Battery, which had amazingly been refitted with volunteers from the infantry in the fourteen days since the Battle of Iuka. Realizing that the battery was about to be attacked by the exact regiments that had nearly annihilated it two weeks prior, Lt. Henry Neil called out to his men, "Boys, there are the same troops that fought us at Iuka; are you going to let them touch our guns today?" Neil later remarked that "the yell of rage that went up was more ominous than a rebel yell ever tried to be." As the gray lines advanced into the maelstrom of lead, the Ohio cannoneers screamed with rage, "Come on! if you think you can play Iuka again!" The Union guns cut the Confederates to pieces. Colonel McLain was severely wounded while leading the assault, and both brigades were hurled back with heavy losses. After the war, Lieutenant Neil would proudly state that "the men worked like tigers in

A picture of the defenses of Corinth taken after the battle. Battery Williams is located on the left of the tracks, and on the right the earthworks of Battery Robinette are visible behind the tents. *Francis Miller's Photographic History of the Civil War.*

their desperate resolve that their beloved guns would never again feel the insult of a rebel touch. . . . they came so close that we resorted to double charges of canister and never a rebel reached the muzzles of our guns."[11]

Federal reserves from Sullivan's brigade, now under the command of Col. Samuel Holmes, rushed into the breach at Battery Powell. The remaining Rebels were forced to retreat out of the stronghold into the open ground they had previously advanced across. Gates's men neglected to carry tools with them to spike the fort's cannon, and the Missourians were slaughtered when the Northerners fired the pieces into the backs of the retreating Confederates. After Gates withdrew, Brig. Gen. W.L. Cabell's brigade from Maury's division appeared to exploit the now terminated breakthrough. Delayed by a communications error, Cabell arrived expecting to complete the drive into Corinth, but discovered to his horror that Battery Powell was back in the hands of the Union. Too late to aid the Missourians, Cabell nonetheless assaulted the battery, and in intense fighting, lost almost half of his brigade before disengaging. Green, by hitting Davies's division, had the best chance to tear the Union line apart, but a lack of necessary reserves doomed the attack before it began. Confederate James Payne described the bloodstained appearance of survivors as "men came out of that storm looking like workers in an abattoir."[12]

As the sun climbed higher in the sky, the temperature rose steadily to 94 degrees, and the epicenter of Van Dorn's desperate endeavor shifted to the right. At 11:00 A.M., Major Gen. Dabney Maury commenced his assault on the Union fortifications centered around Battery Robinette. Maury's two brigades, under brigadier generals John C. Moore and C.W. Phifer, would attack the most elaborate defenses Rosecrans had constructed at Corinth. The Southerners would have to advance 250 yards under the vicious fire of the three 20 lbs. Parrott rifles in Battery Robinette and the five 30 lbs. Parrotts in Battery Williams, claw their way through a thick tangle of felled trees, and then finally cross a 100-yard field in front of well prepared earthworks manned by General Stanley's hard fighting Federals. The charge would be made by regiments concentrated in narrow attack columns, with Moore's men stacked behind Phifer's.[13]

At the front of John C. Moore's brigade was the vaunted 2nd Texas Infantry. The 2nd Texas was a tough, veteran unit that contained such notable members as Dr. Ashbel Smith, and until his wounding at Shiloh, Sam Houston, Jr. The Texans had a reputation for ferocity equaled only by that of their commander, Col. William P. Rogers, a prominent lawyer from Mississippi who had migrated to Texas in 1851. During the Mexican War, Rogers held the rank of captain in Jefferson Davis's famed Mississippi Rifles, earning both a stellar combat record and, for reasons unknown, the personal animosity of Davis. In the current war, the lasting feud with the Confederate President denied Rogers a much warranted promotion to general. Determined to earn a higher rank or die in

WILLIAM S. ROGERS

Born in 1819 in Georgia, Rogers grew up on a plantation in Monroe County, Mississippi. After graduating from a medical college in Kentucky, Rogers practiced medicine until an interest in politics inspired him to begin studying law. In 1842, the self-taught Rogers was admitted to the Mississippi state bar and become a professional attorney. During the Mexican War, he was elect-

ed captain of Company K of the First Mississippi Volunteer Infantry, which became the famous "Mississippi Rifles" under Col. Jefferson Davis. Rogers fought with distinction at the battles of Monterrey and Buena Vista, but tension between himself and Davis resulted in a lasting personal dispute. In 1849, thanks largely to his war record, President Zachary Taylor appointed Rogers to the United States Consul at the port of Vera Cruz in Mexico, but Rogers resigned in 1851 after one of his agents was falsely accused of embezzlement. Settling in Texas, Rogers became a prominent lawyer and one of the first professors at Baylor University's Law School. A close friend and supporter of Sam Houston, Rogers became a strong supporter of secession after Abraham Lincoln's election in 1860. Elected as a delegate to the secession convention from Harris County, Rogers unhesitatingly voted for separation and was soon after commis-

sioned as the lieutenant colonel of the 2nd Texas Infantry under Col. John C. Moore. Rogers and the Texans first saw combat at Shiloh in April 1862, where Rogers earned praise for his courageous leadership during the fighting. When Moore was given command of the brigade, Rogers was promoted to colonel of the 2nd Texas. In August, his fellow officers from twenty separate regiments petitioned the Confederate War Department for Rogers's promotion to major general, a request that President Davis refused to act upon. At the Battle of Corinth in October 1862, Rogers led the regiment in a furious attack against the outer defenses of the town on the first day of battle, and on the second day personally led three separate charges upon the almost impregnable Federal fortifications around Battery Robinette. In the third and final assault, Rogers achieved a momentary breakthrough, but was killed by Union reinforcements that quickly overwhelmed his exhausted and bloodied command. Rogers's conspicuous bravery inspired Union Maj. Gen. William S. Rosecrans to order that he be buried with full military honors, and today a marble monument marks his grave in Corinth.

the attempt, Rogers strapped on a vest of body armor and readied his command for the perilous venture.[14]

Behind the Union breastworks, Capt. Oscar L. Jackson of the 63rd Ohio watched the Confederates approach with mounting apprehension. When the thick gray columns emerged from the woods, Jackson noted that "everything was silent as the grave." He later recalled that "I thought they would never stop coming out of the timber. . . . As soon as they were ready they started at us with a firm, slow, steady step. . . . In my campaigning I had never seen anything so hard to stand as that slow, steady tramp." As Maury's men pressed on, Jackson observed that "not a sound was heard but they looked as if they intended to walk over us. I afterwards stood a bayonet charge when the enemy came at us on the double-quick with a yell and it was not so trying on the nerves as that steady, solemn advance." Amazed by the swarm of Rebels drawing ever closer to his position, the Ohio captain declared starkly, "Boys, I guess we are going to have a fight."[15]

Advancing with the 42nd Alabama, Lt. Charles Labruzan recorded that as the men reached "the crest of a hill, the whole of Corinth with its enormous fortifications burst upon our view. The United States flag was floating over the forts and in the town." Instantly, the Union line erupted in a terrific hail of gunfire that staggered the Southerners. Lieutenant Labruzan recounted the devastation, writing that "we were now met by a perfect storm of grape, canister, cannon and minie balls. Oh! God, I never saw the like. The men fell like grass." Alongside the Ohioans, Capt. Oscar Jackson testified that "as the smoke cleared away, there was apparently ten yards square of a mass of struggling bodies and butternut clothes. Their column appeared to reel like a rope shaken at the end."[16]

The reduced Confederates pushed on resolutely into the deadly tempest. Charging with his Alabamians, Labruzan reported that "I saw men running at full speed, stop suddenly and fall on their faces, with their brains scattered all around; others with legs or arms cut off, shrieking with agony. . . . The ground was literally strewn with mangled corpses." Halted by the intense fire of the forts, Maury's men were forced to fall back from the Federal inferno. Stubbornly, the Rebels reformed their ranks and advanced once again against Battery Robinette, this time at the double quick. The results were the same as before. In his account, Jackson stated that "they dashed themselves against us like water against a rock and were a second time repulsed and gave back."[17]

The two bloody assaults had taken their toll on Stanley's Federals as well. In the 63rd Ohio, Captain Jackson's company was ordered to relieve another company posted to the right of Robinette. He later related that "it was like moving into dead men's shoes, for I had seen one company carried away from there on litters, but without hesitation we moved up." Incredibly, the surviving soldiers in gray were able to rally for a third attack. As John C. Moore's men moved up past Phifer's shattered ranks, Colonel Rogers rode up to his men and yelled "Forward, Texans!" Rogers led the charge on horseback, riding forward while waving the colors of the 2nd Texas. Captain Jackson illustrated the intensity of the moment when he later wrote, "the Texans began yelling like savages and rushed at us without firing." The Southerners dashed up to the ditch in front of Battery Robinette at a dead run, and fought a furious close quarter battle with the 1st U.S. Infantry inside. The two sides blazed away at one another at point blank range over the seven foot high walls of the battery. Lieutenant Labruzan recalled that "a man within two feet of me put his head cautiously up to shoot into the fort, but suddenly dropped his musket, and his brains were dashed in a stream over my fine coat, which I had in my arms."[18]

The carnage was almost beyond comprehension. The Federals threw hand grenades down into the ditch filled with Confederates, who quickly began hurling them back into

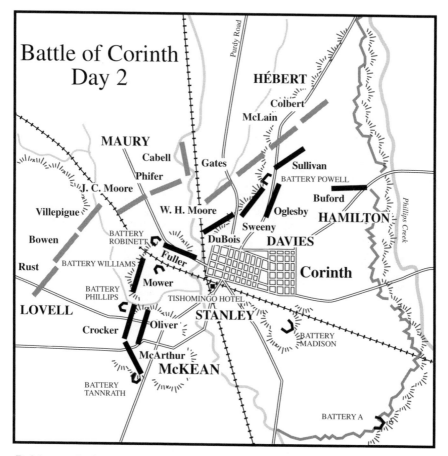

Battle of Corinth
Day 2

Robinette before they exploded. One eyewitness stated that "it seemed as though hell was holding jubilee." Rogers' men stormed the parapets and plunged into a fierce hand-to-hand struggle for the fort. Watching the mêlée from a distance, Union Lt. Cyrus Boyd recorded that "it was a bloody contest and we could see men using their bayonets like pitch forks, and thrusting each other through." Rogers' men seized control of the battery for a brief moment, but then were struck by a ferocious counterattack led by the 11th Missouri and 27th Ohio. Caught by surprise, the Texans and Alabamians were cut down like victims of a firing squad. Colonel Rogers fell dead

A *Harper's Weekly* illustration of the struggle for Battery Robinette, from the November 1, 1862 issue.

alongside his horse, his armored vest pierced with seven bullet holes. Lieutenant Labruzan later recalled the bloodshed: "we were butchered like dogs, as we were not supported. . . . The men fell ten at a time. The ditch being full, and finding that we had no chance, we the survivors, tried to save ourselves as best we could."[19]

The few men left standing in Maury's two brigades raced back across the open field to Confederate lines, under a brutal cannonade from the guns inside Battery Robinette. Lieutenant Labruzan remembered that "just then I saw poor Foster throw up his hands and saying 'Oh, my God!' jumped about two feet off the ground and fell on his face. The top of his head seemed to cave in, and the blood spouted straight up several feet." The Rebel officer further stated that "I could see men falling as they attempted to run; some with their heads blown to pieces and others with the blood streaming from their backs. It was horrible." Many Southerners were captured, including Labruzan. In his account of the futile attack, he admitted that "for the first time in many years, I cried to see our brave men slaughtered so. I have never felt so bad in all my life." A Texan in Phifer's brigade recounted that "our long columns of solders [*sic*] rolled back from the deadly strife of death, leaving perhaps half of their men wounded, prisoners and dead upon the field. This was war to the knife. In places you could walk on the dead."[20]

After the battle, Cyrus Boyd commented that "although they are enemies of our government and our flag I could not help but *pity* these poor fellows who thus went into *certain* and *sure destruction* here." Reflecting upon the charge, he remarked that "they had been *cut to pieces* in the most intense meaning of that term. Such bravery has never been excelled on any field as the useless assaults on Robinette." General Rosecrans witnessed the onslaught of Colonel Rogers and was astounded by the courage of the Southerners. He went so far as to name Rogers and the 2nd Texas in his report, and after the war he declared that the attack "was about as good fighting on the part of the Confederates as I ever saw."[21]

Along the Union earthworks to the right of Battery Robinette, a few members of W.H. Moore's brigade and Maury's division managed to slice through the Federals in Col. John Du Bois's brigade of Davies's division. Around two thousand screaming Rebels streamed into the streets of Corinth and swept past the large, two-story Tishomingo Hotel. Fighting from house to house, the Confederates chased the Union troops across the railroad tracks and seized Rosecrans's headquarters. Rosecrans rode into the midst of the fray, rallying his men with a frenzy of curses and commands. The reckless effort was nearly fatal for "Old Rosy," as he acknowledged that, "my *sabre-tasche* strap was cut by a bullet, and my gloves were stained with the blood of a staff-officer wounded at my side." At one point, Rosecrans spied a large number of Confederates sheltered on the porch of a house. He directed a two-gun battery to pour canister into the Southerners and reported that "after one round, only the dead and dying were left on the porch." The urban combat raged bitterly without either side gaining an advantage, and as one Yankee expressed it, "consternation reigned supreme." Finally, in a savage counterattack, the 17th Iowa and the 5th Minnesota drove the Confederates out of the town. Some of the Southerners escaped by riding horses they appropriated from the Tishomingo Hotel, but most of the survivors were captured. By 1:00 P.M., the battle of Corinth was over.[22]

On Van Dorn's far right flank, the men of Lovell's division waited for orders to move forward in support of Price's brigades. The order never arrived. Maj. Gen. Mansfield Lovell took one look at the Federal fortifications around Battery Philips and decided he wanted nothing to do with them. Lovell's inactivity forever infuriated Price's men, who were massacred while Van Dorn's own division stood idly by. In all probability, however, an attack by Lovell would have accomplished little more than to add to the already tremendous amount of Confederate dead and wounded. When an aide asked General Bowen what would happen if he was forced to assault Battery Philips, Bowen bleakly responded, "my brigade will march up and be killed."[23]

As the defeated remnants of his division limped back into the trees, Dabney Maury confessed that "it was not in any man's power to form them into line." Maury was present as Sterling Price rode out among the broken ranks, and recalled that the Missourian "looked on the disorder of his daring troops with unmitigated anguish." Maury observed that "the big tears coursed down the old man's bronzed face, and I have never witnessed such a picture of mute despair and grief as his countenance wore when he looked upon the utter defeat of those magnificent troops. He had never before known them to fail."[24]

Kurz & Allison's 1891 lithograph of the Battle of Corinth, depicting the charge of the 2d Texas Infantry at Battery Robinette. *Courtesy of Mississippi Department of Archives and History.*

Nearby, Maury noted that General Van Dorn "looked upon the thousands of men streaming past him with a mingled expression of sorrow and pity." His grand charge for glory had turned into a worse disaster than Pea Ridge. Maury stated that "never was a general more disappointed than Van Dorn; but no man in all our army was so little shaken in his courage by the result as he was." Realizing that his long-awaited redemption was lost, Van Dorn reluctantly ordered a withdrawal and directed Lovell's division to act as rear guard. Remembering the moment, Maury later recalled "however much depression all of us showed and felt, he alone remained unconquered, and if he could have gotten his forces together would have tried it again." At the same time, unknown to Van Dorn, General Grant's troops were marching hard to complete the victory at Corinth by cutting off the Confederate retreat. Once again, Grant would have the opportunity to destroy a large southern army, and he was determined not to let the Rebels slip away this time.[25]

7

"GIT OUT O' THAR TAIL-END FIRST"

After the battle had ended, Maj. Gen. William S. Rosecrans rode out along his lines to Battery Robinette. The area around the fort was littered with the human wreckage of Van Dorn's futile assaults, piled in what Lt. Cyrus Boyd described as "heaps of slain." Realizing that his former pupil, Dabney Maury, had commanded the division that attacked Robinette, Rosecrans remarked, "I never used to think when I taught him, a little curly-headed boy at West Point, that he would ever trouble me as he has to-day." False rumors of Rosecrans's death had permeated the Federal ranks, and his unharmed appearance was greeted by thunderous cheers from the victorious blue army. After Rosecrans congratulated the men for their triumph, Boyd noted that "the wildest enthusiasm prevailed and every man seems ready to pursue the enemy[.] We have had but few battles so well managed as old 'Rosa' has managed this one."[1]

JAMES B. MCPHERSON

Born in Ohio in 1828, McPherson graduated from the U.S. Military Academy in 1853, first in his class of fifty-two that included J.B. Hood, P.H. Sheridan, and J.M. Schofield. Commissioned a 2d lieutenant of engineers, he taught at the academy and worked on coastal fortifications. He was promoted to 1st lieutenant in 1858 and captain in August 1861. He retained his staff assignment following the outbreak of the Civil War. He was promoted to lieutenant colonel in November 1861, and assigned as aide-de-camp to Gen. Henry Halleck in Missouri. He was Gen. U.S. Grant's chief engineer during the battles at Forts Henry and Donelson, Shiloh, and in the advance on Corinth. Promoted to colonel in May 1862, he entered the volunteer organization that same month as brigadier general. He commanded the Engineer Brigade, Army of the Tennessee, until his promotion to major general of volunteers in October 1862. He commanded the Seventeenth Corps, Army of the Tennessee, during the Vicksburg Campaign and was promoted to brigadier general in the regular army in August 1863. He led his corps in the Meridian Campaign and in March 1864 succeeded Gen. W.T. Sherman as commander of the

Department and Army of the Tennessee. He led the army, one of three in Sherman's conglomerate force, during the early stages of the Atlanta Campaign, but his indecisive actions at Snake Creek Gap in May and during the Battle of Peachtree Creek in July led to missed opportunities to crush the Confederate army. During the Battle of Atlanta in July 1864, General McPherson was killed by Rebel skirmishers as he rode unescorted to the scene of the fighting. A particular favorite of both Grant and Sherman, he was a loyal and dependable subordinate; as an army commander, however, he proved unequal to the responsibility.

Early that evening, Brig. Gen. James McPherson arrived in Corinth with a brigade of fresh troops and new instructions from Grant. Rosecrans was ordered to chase after the Confederates in coordination with Hurlbut's thrust from

Bolivar, in order to trap Van Dorn along the swampy banks of the Hatchie River. Well aware that both he and his army were hungry, thirsty, and completely worn out from two days of intense fighting under grueling conditions, Rosecrans decided to wait until the following day to begin the pursuit. He rested his soldiers and prepared to move out at dawn.[2]

Disappointed but still defiant, Confederate Maj. Gen. Earl Van Dorn spent the rest of October 4 leading his defeated army back along the same road that they had marched over so hopefully only two days before. To the surprise of his subordinates, Van Dorn directed his men to halt for the night at Chewalla, rather than pressing on the four remaining miles past the strong natural defenses of the Tuscumbia River. When his perplexed division commanders inquired as to why the retreat was halted so near to the vital bridge, Van Dorn calmly informed them that the Army of West Tennessee was not returning to Ripley, but redeploying instead to Rienzi in order to assault Corinth from the south. The officers were incredulous. Brig. Gen. Dabney Maury recalled that "the utmost depression prevailed throughout the army, and it was with no elation we heard our dauntless leader, Van Dorn, had determined to make another attack that day on the enemy at Rienzi."[3]

Maj. Gen. Sterling Price, well aware that such a misadventure was madness, speculated that the scheme indicated a "mind rendered desperate by misfortune." Along with the rest of the army's senior leadership, Price pointed out the impossibility of the proposed offensive to the commanding general. Another bold dissenter stated bluntly that, "Van Dorn, you are the only man I ever saw who loves danger for its own sake. When any daring enterprise is before you, you cannot adequately estimate the obstacles in your way." Van Dorn, recognizing that he faced the real possibility of a mutiny, responded that, "while I do not admit the correctness of your criticism, I feel how wrong I shall be to imperil this army through my personal peculiarities . . . I will countermand the orders and move at once on the road to Ripley."[4]

On October 5, Grant confidently informed Halleck that "at this distance everything looks favorable, and I cannot see how the enemy are to escape without losing everything but their small-arms. I have strained everything to take into the fight an adequate force and to get them to the right place." That morning, however, Rosecrans's planned pursuit quickly disintegrated into a comedy of errors. McPherson, who was supposed to be in the lead, apparently misunderstood his orders and did not get started until well after sunrise. Brig. Gen. Charles Hamilton wandered his division down the wrong road and collided with the divisions of brigadier generals David Stanley and Thomas A. Davies. In return, Stanley and Davies turned their men around and took the road reserved for Hamilton, which took them straight into the rear of Brig. Gen. Thomas J. McKean's unhurried division. McKean had for some reason persuaded himself that he needed to bring his mile-long wagon train along, which slowed the Federal march to a crawl. Eventually, all four Union division commanders became embroiled in a heated argument while their men languished under the blistering sun in a nightmarish traffic jam. In the end, Rosecrans had to intervene and settle the dispute from his headquarters in Corinth in order to finally get the pursuit moving.[5]

Well ahead of the embarrassing quagmire, General McPherson actually caught up with and engaged the southern rear guard, but a spirited action by Confederate Brig. Gen. John Bowen's brigade prevented McPherson from achieving anything of consequence. Federal Brig. Gen. John McArthur managed to avoid the chaos only to be delayed by a large body of Southerners dispatched by Van Dorn to request permission to properly dispose of their dead comrades at Corinth. The hard-charging Scotsman wasted three hours negotiating with the delegation, which McPherson had wisely bypassed and

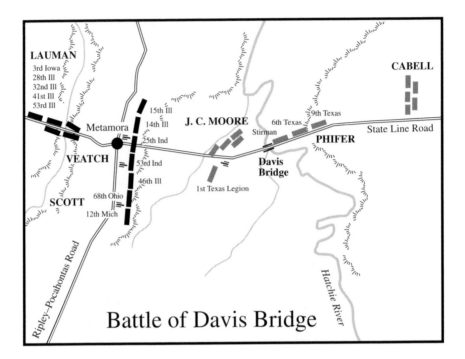

Battle of Davis Bridge

ignored. The time consumed by the senseless parley precluded any possibility of McArthur threatening Van Dorn's ravaged army before sunset. In the midst of McArthur's column was Cyrus Boyd, who observed that "the roadside for miles was lined with abandoned wagons [and] dead and wounded Rebs. . . . Saw sixteen dead in one place[.] They lay like sheaves of grain ready to be shocked. . . . The panic has been an awful one."[6]

The other wing of Grant's intended pincer movement enjoyed somewhat more success. At 9:00 A.M. on October 5 the five thousand Northerners under Maj. Gen. Stephen Hurlbut reached the lightly defended Davis Bridge, Van Dorn's critical crossing over the Hatchie River. Before Hurlbut could launch his attack, Maj. Gen. Edward O.C. Ord overtook the Bolivar detachment and assumed command. A stunned Van Dorn was now forced to call upon the only troops he had

Stephen Hurlbut

Born in Charleston, South Carolina, in 1815, Hurlbut was the son of a transplanted New England Unitarian minister. After passing the South Carolina bar, Hurlbut opened a law practice in Charleston and in 1840 became an adjutant in a South Carolina militia unit that served during the Second Seminole War. In 1845, charges of fraud forced him to resettle in Belvidare, Illinois, where he again practiced law and gained influence in the Whig Party. In 1847, Hurlbut was elected to the state constitutional convention and in 1848 served as a presidential elector. As the Whig Party declined in the 1850s, Hurlbut joined the new Republican Party and served in the state legislature from 1858 until the outbreak of the Civil War. Due to his political connections with fellow Illinois Republican Abraham Lincoln, Hurlbut was commissioned as a brigadier general on June 14, 1861. After serving briefly in Illinois and Missouri, Hurlbut was given command of a brigade in Ulysses S. Grant's Army of the Tennessee which he led through the campaign against Forts Henry and Donelson. Shortly thereafter he was placed in command of the 4th Division, which he led with distinction at the Battle of Shiloh. On September 17, 1862, Hurlbut was promoted to  major general and led a sizable force against the Confederate offensive to recapture Corinth, Mississippi, and was bloodily repulsed at the battle of Davis Bridge. Subsequently appointed commander of the District of Memphis, he resigned after the fall of Vicksburg, assuming the war would soon end. When it became apparent that he was mistaken, Hurlbut decided to remain in the Army and spent the next nine months attempting in vain to defeat the vaunted Confederate cavalry commander Nathan Bedford Forrest. After failing to destroy Forrest, and being surrounded by allegations of drunkenness and cotton smuggling, General Sherman removed Hurlbut from command in April 1864. After a brief assignment in Illinois, he replaced Nathaniel Banks as commander of the Department of the Gulf in September 1864, where Hurlbut would remain until the end of the war. Headquartered in New Orleans, Hurlbut soon ran afoul of Washington by criticizing the Lincoln appointed occupation government and continuing his cotton smuggling operations. In 1865, an investigation recommended his arrest, but Republican officials feared the effects of a political scandal and allowed Hurlbut to leave the army without penalty. Returning to Illinois, he resumed his political career, serving again in the state legislature and as the first commander of the Grand Army of the Republic, where he was again accused of drunkenness and corruption. In 1869, President Grant appointed him U.S. Minister to Colombia, and after two terms in the House of Representatives, President Garfield selected Hurlbut to be Minister to Peru, where Hurlbut violated U.S. neutrality by supporting Peru during the War of the Pacific. Hurlbut died in Lima in 1882 and is buried in Belvedere, Illinois.

nearby, the remnants of Maury's crippled division, to hold back the approaching Union troops. Maury, after being warned by Van Dorn that "you are in for it again to day," dispatched the three hundred remaining men of Moore's brigade, along with the 1st Texas Legion, across the bridge to stall the Federal advance.[7]

The situation was desperate. If Ord could secure the crossing, the Confederates would be trapped between two converging Union armies. One Missourian later recounted that a friend's battle cry at Iuka had been "victory or crippled," which was revised at Corinth to "victory or death." When asked of his new slogan before the swarming blue multitude at Davis Bridge, the disenchanted Rebel replied, "there's no motto for this place—I can only say, we all thought Van Dorn played hell at Elkhorn, and now he has done it, sure enough."[8]

Ord's brigades quickly overwhelmed Moore's exhausted men in the open fields before the bridge, capturing four cannon and hundreds of Confederates cornered along the river bank. The jubilant Federals rushed across the bridge to complete the rout, but were stopped cold by the rest of Maury's division deployed along a heavily forested and naturally defensible ridge. Maury's thin gray line consisted of perhaps 1,000-1,500 worn-out men who had only the day before endured some of the most horrific combat of the entire war. They were now the only force available to prevent the complete rout of Van Dorn's army. Supported by three artillery batteries, the depleted Confederates unleashed a stunningly effective fire of canister and minie balls that severely punished the attacking Federals and cut down over five hundred Union soldiers in roughly four hours of fighting. Ord fell with a serious leg wound and was replaced by Hurlbut, and the Union attack bogged down in the Mississippi mud. One Southerner remarked that, "I never saw such slaughter in my life. They fell by the hundred, then recoiled, reformed and rushed to meet the same result. It was impossible to drive us from that position by direct assault."

Eventually Hurlbut flanked Maury's position and drove the Confederates away, but the bloodied Northerners lacked the strength to push further. Nevertheless, Van Dorn had lost his only crossing over the wide Hatchie River, and unless fortune intervened, his complete destruction would be only a matter of time.[9]

Miraculously, Van Dorn learned from his cavalry that a damaged but viable bridge still spanned the river at Crum's Mill, six miles below Davis Bridge. A member of Col. Elijah Gates brigade recalled that "we were saved by the hot haste of a jaunty aid[e], who came rushing frantically from the jaunty Van Dorn, with orders to move by the left flank, which meant, as I heard one of the men explain, 'git out o' thar tail-end first.'" During the night, under the energetic direction of General Price, the Army of West Tennessee crossed the Hatchie and escaped the Union snare.[10]

Frustrated once again, a disgusted Grant ordered the pursuit to be called off on October 7. Rosecrans, realizing that Van Dorn's command was near collapse, answered in a long-winded and impassioned protest, stating: "I most deeply dissent from your views as to the manner of pursuing. We have defeated, routed, and demoralized the army which holds the Lower Mississippi Valley. . . . All that is needful is to continue pursuing and whip them." Rosecrans could see no reason to turn back, but he dramatically affirmed that "if, after considering these matters, you still consider the order for my return to Corinth expedient I will obey it and abandon the chief fruits of a victory." When Grant notified Halleck of his decision to end the chase, even "Old Brains" inquired, "why order a return of our troops? Why not re-enforce Rosecrans and pursue the enemy into Mississippi, supporting your army on the country?"[11]

The truth was that Grant had been singularly unimpressed with Rosecrans's slow start to pursue Van Dorn after the battle, and had simply lost all confidence in "Old Rosy's" ability to

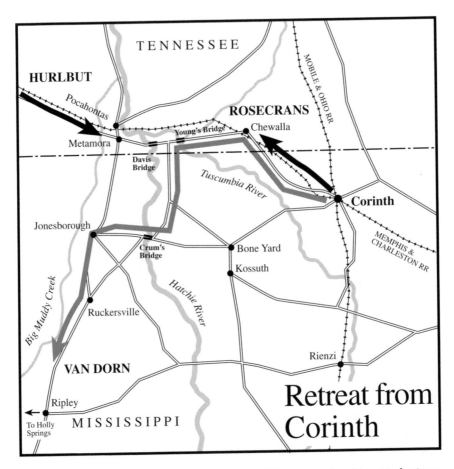

Retreat from Corinth

command. Grant had seen two golden opportunities to destroy Confederate armies slip through his fingers at Iuka and Davis Bridge, and he placed the majority of the blame on Rosecrans. Grant felt that he could no longer rely upon his temperamental subordinate and refused to risk the Federal army in a continued advance. This was a rare display of hesitation from Grant, who had witnessed firsthand Halleck's blundering in May that allowed Beauregard to save and rebuild the Confederate army after the siege of Corinth. Rosecrans would rage over the recall for the rest of his career, fuming that "if Grant had not stopped us, we could have gone to Vicksburg." Confederate Gen. Danbey Maury agreed, writing after the war that "the enemy remained supine, and for more than a month we were encamped about Holly Springs, and actively engaged in reorganizing, refitting, and reinforcing our army. A vigorous pursuit immediately after our defeat at Corinth would have prevented all this and effectually destroyed our whole command."[12]

During the withdrawal, straggling and desertion reached epidemic proportions in Van Dorn's army. Tired of being poorly supplied and ineptly led, many discontented soldiers simply disappeared into the trees and went home. The 35th Mississippi was reduced to a mere skeleton of its former self, mustering only one officer and forty men after the flight at Crum's bridge. One Mississippian bitterly complained that the "retreat was characterized by all the mismanagement of the advance and attack on Corinth. No rations were ever issued to the worn-out soldier, and what we lived on was taken from the citizens living on the line of retreat, most of the time at night." Another soldier in gray lamented that "our retreat was conducted with the greatest confusion and Van Dorn was drunk all the time and Villipigue too and I expect Price too. . . . We lost half of Price's army killed and *straggling*. Such demoralization was never seen in an army before."[13]

The campaign for Corinth took a bloody toll on both sides. Rosecrans reported 355 men killed, 1,841 wounded, and 324 missing in the battle, and Hurlbut lost another 570 dead and wounded in the scuffle at Davis Bridge. Exact Confederate losses are unknown, but are estimated to be around 505 men killed, 2,150 wounded, and 2,183 missing at Corinth, with a further 400-500 men lost at Davis Bridge, mostly captured. Confederate casualties were heavily concentrated in Price's corps, which endured the worst fighting on the second day. Brig. Gen. John C. Moore's brigade, which spearheaded the assault on Battery Robinette, was nearly annihilated, losing 1,295 of its 1,892 men. The Federal dead were buried in what

The bodies of fallen Confederates, collected for burial near Battery Robinette on October 5, 1862. In the foreground on the far left is Col. Rogers. *Library of Congress.*

would later become Corinth National Cemetery, while the Rebel fatalities were buried in unmarked mass graves. Only Col. William Rogers, of the 2nd Texas Infantry, received a proper burial. Rosecrans was so impressed by Rogers's courage during the assault on Battery Robinette that he ordered Rogers' body be buried with full military honors, a rare tribute for a fallen enemy.[14]

Hundreds of miles away in Kentucky, Gen. Braxton Bragg continued his offensive, fighting the Federals to a draw in the battle of Perryville on October 8. Four days later he received word of Van Dorn's catastrophe at Corinth, destroying any hopes he had of receiving reinforcements from Mississippi. An aide recorded that "his mind was immediately made up. The cause of the whole country required that he should return and that the fate of the whole Confederacy should not be staked upon an unequal engagement with the enemy, nor by the dangers of delay." Bragg's decision to abandon Kentucky, combined with the repulse of Robert E. Lee's incursion into Maryland, gave the North continental success against the coordinated Confederate offensives. Never again would the South attempt anything so bold, and never again would the Confederacy come so close to winning independence.[15]

In his memoirs, Gen. William T. Sherman wrote that the Battle of Corinth was "a decisive blow to the Confederate cause in our quarter, and changed the whole aspect of affairs in West Tennessee. . . . In Memphis I could see its effects upon the citizens, and they openly admitted that their cause had sustained a death-blow." A devastated Southerner wrote to his wife that "I think the cause of the Confederacy is lost in this West. . . . I am almost in despair as regards our cause. . . . I tell you Sarah that I am whipped now." Weakened by the attrition of Corinth, the South lost the strategic initiative in the Mississippi Valley, and was forced to resort to a desperate defense that could not stand long against the persistent pounding of Ulysses S. Grant.[16]

After Corinth, President Davis elevated Lt. Gen. John C. Pemberton to command of the Department of Mississippi and East Louisiana, replacing Van Dorn with a more cautious administrator. In early November, a humiliated Van Dorn was forced to defend his actions during the battle in a formal court of inquiry. The court found the defendant not guilty of all charges, which prompted a joyful Van Dorn to publish and circulate one thousand copies of the court's report. He later wrote to his wife that "I unhesitatingly say that the attack on Corinth was the best thing I ever did in my life." Once the court disbanded, Van Dorn was transferred to commanding a division of cavalry, where his reckless daring proved to be an asset. In December, he destroyed the Federal supply depot at Holly Springs, which ended Grant's first thrust toward

A picture of the bloody aftermath of the carnage around Battery Robinette, taken the day after the battle. The body of Col. William Rogers can be seen lying on the left of the stump in the center of the picture, and on the right is the colonel's dead horse. *Library of Congress.*

Vicksburg, and in March 1863 he won an impressive victory at Thompson's Station, fighting alongside the legendary Confederate cavalry leader Brig. Gen. Nathan Bedford Forrest. The repeated successes enabled Van Dorn to restore some measure of honor to his name, but a jealous competition for glory, reminiscent of his earlier rivalry with Sterling Price, brought him into a precarious confrontation with the ferocious General Forrest.[17]

After the battle of Thompson's Station, Van Dorn and Forrest became involved in a personal quarrel over Forrest receiving the majority of the accolades for the victory in the press, and his improper distribution of captured arms. In a private meeting, Van Dorn boldly accused that a member of Forrest's staff was writing articles for the *Chattanooga Rebel.* Forrest, infuriated at the allegation, fiercely declared that, "I know nothing of the articles you refer to, and I demand from you your authority for this assertion. I shall hold him responsible and make him eat his words, or run my sabre through him; and I say to you as well, that I will hold you personally responsible if you do not produce the author." Van Dorn, realizing that his bluff was called, remarked to an aide that, "I do not assert, nor do I believe, that General Forrest inspired those articles, or had any knowledge of them." This retraction pacified the hot-tempered Tennessean, who responded, "General Van Dorn and I have enough to do fighting the enemies of our country without fighting each other." The two commanders reconciled, and it appeared that Van Dorn's fortunes were finally turning for the better.[18]

But the handsome general's luck had run out. On May 6, 1863, Van Dorn was murdered by Dr. George Peters for allegedly cavorting with Mrs. Peters while the doctor was out of town. Ironically, before his death Van Dorn was advised by a wise Tennessee widow to "let the women alone until the war is over." Without hesitation, Van Dorn responded, "My God, Madam! I cannot do that, for it is all I am fighting for. I hate all men, and were it not for the women, I should not fight at all; besides, if I accepted your generous advice, I would not now be speaking to you." Unfortunately for the South, Van Dorn's natural talent for leading cavalry was overlooked for the majority of his career, and he instead wasted priceless resources and lives proving that he was unsuited for army command.[19]

After Van Dorn's untimely demise, one of his cavalrymen wrote in his diary that "a universal gloom cast over the troops—now [we] begin to feel his real worth," while another called the murder "one of the severest blows to the Confederacy." Van Dorn's assassination did not elicit sympathy from the infantry who had survived the butchery of Corinth. One disillusioned Southerner wrote home that "infamy & shame have blackened his fame; and shame & regret are all he transmits to his posterity. He sealed with his death the shameful name which he had acquired in life, namely that of a vile seducer." A Texan stated starkly that "the Army nor humanity lost nothing."[20]

In February 1863, Gen. Sterling Price finally received his long-awaited reassignment to the Trans-Mississippi theater. Given command of troops in Arkansas. In 1864, he led a small army into Missouri, hoping to finally liberate his home state. But his dreams of a Confederate Missouri were extinguished in defeat, and for the last time he barely escaped destruction from the Federals to retreat back into Arkansas. His beloved Missourians stayed in Mississippi, never having received permission to cross back over the river. Instead they remained in the Western Theater, serving at Vicksburg and then with the Army of Tennessee until the end of the war.[21]

On October 23, General Rosecrans was selected by Halleck to replace Maj. Gen. Don Carlos Buell as the commander of the Army of the Ohio, which Rosecrans renamed the Army of the Cumberland. Grant later admitted that "I was delighted at the promotion of General Rosecrans to a separate command. . . . As a subordinate I found that I could not make him do as I wished, and had determined to relieve him from duty that very day." The relationship between Grant and Rosecrans never healed, and they would remain hostile to one another for the rest of their lives.[22]

Grant, freed from the doubt and suspicion of his superiors, prepared to finish the conquest he had begun with the capture of Forts Henry and Donelson. After the war he wrote that the Battle of Corinth "relieved me from any further anxiety for the safety of the territory within my jurisdiction, and soon after receiving reinforcements I suggested to the general-in-chief a forward movement against Vicksburg." Triumphant over his enemies, both blue and gray, Ulysses S. Grant had developed into the commander that would eventually win the war for the North. With customary resolve, Grant turned his attention southward, and started on the long road that would take him down the river to Vicksburg and then to the war's end with Lee's surrender at Appomattox.[23]

"What of them is left, to tell
Where they lie, and how they fell?
Not a stone on their turf, nor a bone in their graves;
But they live in the verse that immortality saves.

...

Thus was Corinth lost and won!"
—Lord Byron, *The Siege of Corinth*

NOTES

1. "Hell or Corinth"

1   Kristy Armstrong White, "Life in Civil War Tishomingo County, Mississippi" (M.A. thesis, Mississippi State University, 1998), 21; William S. Rosecrans, "The Battle of Corinth," *Battles and Leaders of the Civil War*, Robert Underwood Johnson and Clarence Clough Buel, eds. (New York: Castle Books, 1956), 738-40.

2   White, "Life in Civil War," 6-10.

3   R.S. Bevier, *History of the First and Second Missouri Confederate Brigades: 1861-1865 and From Wakarusa to Appomattox, A Military Anagraph* (St. Louis, Mo.: Bryan, Brand, & Company, 1879), 325; White, "Life in Civil War," 5; Rosecrans, "Battle of Corinth," 740.

4   Shelby Foote, *The Civil War: A Narrative, Fort Sumter to Perryville* (New York: Random House, Inc., 1958), 168-76.

5   Ibid., 176-80; William C. Davis, Brian C. Pohanka, and Don Troiani, eds., *Civil War Journal: The Leaders* (Nashville, Tenn.: Rutledge Hill Press, 1997), 183-92.

6   Quoted in Edward H. Bonekemper III, *A Victor, Not A Butcher: Ulysses S. Grant's Overlooked Military Genius* (Washington, D.C.: Regnery Publishing, Inc., 2004), 14; Spencer C. Tucker, *Unconditional Surrender: the Capture of Forts Henry and Donelson* (Abilene, Tex.: McWhiney Foundation Press, 2001), 13-30, 104-105.

7   Foote, *The Civil War*, 173.

8   *The War of the Rebellion: A Compilation of the Official Records of the Union and Confederate Armies* (Washington, D.C., 1880-1901), vol. VII part I, 627-28. Hereinafter cited as *OR*; Peter Cozzens, *The Darkest Days of the War: The Battles of Iuka and Corinth* (Chapel Hill, N.C.: University of North Carolina Press, 1997), 13-17.

9   Foote, *The Civil War*, 320-24.

10 Ibid., 351, 373-77.

11 Cyrus F. Boyd, *The Civil War Diary of Cyrus F. Boyd: Fifteenth Iowa Infantry 1861-1863*, Mildred Throne, ed. (Millwood, N.Y.: Kraus Reprint Co., 1977), 47; Albert Marrin, *Unconditional Surrender: U.S. Grant and the Civil War* (New York: Atheneum Macmillan Publishing Co., 1994), 75; Ulysses S. Grant, *Memoirs and Selected Letters: Personal Memoirs of U.S. Grant, Selected Letters 1839-1865*, Mary Drake McFeely and William S. McFeely, eds., (New York: The Library of America, 1990), 1007-1008; Geoffrey Perret, *Ulysses S. Grant: Soldier & President* (New York: Random House, Inc., 1997), 208.

12 Grant, *Memoirs*, 251.

13 Bonekemper, *A Victor, Not A Butcher*, 60-61.

14 Sam R. Watkins, *Co. Aytch* (Jackson, Tenn.: McCowat-Mercer Press, 1952), 71; Foote, *The Civil War*, 381-83.

15 S.B. Barron, *The Lone Star Defenders: A Chronicle of the Third Texas Cavalry, Ross' Brigade* (New York: The Neale Publishing Co., 1908), 89; Lawrence Sullivan Ross, *Personal Civil War Letters of General Lawrence Sullivan Ross: with other letters*, Shelly Morrison, ed. (Austin, Tex.: 1994), 33.

16 Barron, *Lone Star Defenders*, 91.

17 Boyd, *Diary*, 44.

18 *OR*, vol. X part II, 403; Cozzens, *Iuka and Corinth*, 18-19.

19 Dabney Maury, "Recollections of Earl Van Dorn." *Southern Historical Society Papers* vol. XIX (Millwood, N.Y.: Kraus Reprint Co., 1977), 191-201; Arthur B. Carter, *The Tarnished Cavalier: Major General Earl Van Dorn, C.S.A.* (Knoxville, Tenn.: The University of Tennessee Press, 1999), 1-22.

20 Carter, *The Tarnished Cavalier*, 32-33.

21 William L. Shea, *War in the West: Pea Ridge and Prairie Grove* (Abilene, Tex.: McWhiney Foundation Press, 1996), 25-42; Maury, "Recollections of Van Dorn," 194; Kate Cumming, *Kate: The Journal of a Confederate Nurse*, Richard Barksdale Harwell, ed. (Baton Rouge, La.: Louisiana State University Press, 1959), 30; Robert G. Hartje, *Van Dorn: The Life and Times of a Confederate General*, (Nashville, Tenn.: Vanderbilt University Press, 1967), 175.

22 Cumming, *Journal of a Nurse*, 28; Cozzens, *Iuka and Corinth*, 1-5; Albert Castel, *General Sterling Price and the Civil War in the West* (Baton Rouge, La.: Louisiana State University Press, 1968), 85.

23   Barron, *Lone Star Defenders*, 83-84.
24   Foote, *The Civil War*, 370-71; Richmond *Dispatch*, May 30, 1862. 1.
25   Boyd, *Diary*, 52; Cumming, *Journal of a Nurse*, 23.
26   Foote, *The Civil War*, 383-85; *OR*, vol. X part II, 225.
27   Leib Ambrose, *History of the Seventh Regiment Illinois Volunteer Infantry, from its first muster into the U.S. Service, April 25, 1862 to its final muster out, July 9, 1865* (Springfield, Ill.: Illinois Journal Company, 1868), 78.
28   Watkins, *Co. Aytch*, 75; Cozzins, *Iuka and Corinth*, 1-12.
29   Ephraim Anderson, *Memoirs: Historical and Personal: Including the Campaigns of the First Missouri Confederate Brigade* (St. Louis, Mo.: Times Printing Co., 1868), 203.
30   Bevier, *History of the Missouri Brigades*, 329.
31   Barron, *Lone Star Defenders*, 90.
32   *OR*, vol. X part II, 252; Grant, *Memoirs*, 256-57; Oscar L. Jackson., *The Colonel's Diary*, David Prentice, ed. (Sharon, Penn.: 1922), 60.
33   Grant, *Memoirs*, 258; William T. Sherman, *Memoirs of General W.T. Sherman*, Charles Royster, ed. (New York: The Library of America, 1990), 275-76.

2. "The most anxious period of the war"

1   William M. Lamers, *The Edge of Glory: A Biography of General William S. Rosecrans, U.S.A.* (New York: Harcourt, Brace & World, Inc., 1961), 8-19; Peter Cozzens, *The Darkest Days of the War: The Battles of Iuka and Corinth* (Chapel Hill, N.C.: University of North Carolina Press, 1997), 26-28.
2   Lamers, *Edge of Glory*, 20-38.
3   Lamers, *Edge of Glory*, 13, 39-82; Cozzens, *Iuka and Corinth*, 26-29.
4   Shelby Foote, *The Civil War: A Narrative, Fort Sumter to Perryville* (New York: Random House, Inc., 1958), 389-91.
5   Ibid., 392.
6   Ibid., 469-76.
7   Albert Castel, *General Sterling Price and the Civil War in the West* (Baton Rouge, La.: Louisiana State University Press, 1968), 87-88.
8   Castel, *General Sterling Price*, 90; Thomas L. Snead, "With Price East of the Mississippi," *Battles and Leaders of the Civil War: North to Antietam*, Robert Underwood Johnson and Clarence Clough Buel, eds. (New York: Castle Books, 1956), 723-24.
9   Snead, "With Price," 725.
10   Robert G. Hartje, *Van Dorn: The Life and Times of a Confederate General*, (Nashville, Tenn.: Vanderbilt University Press, 1967), 185-95.
11   Hartje, *Van Dorn*, 197-99; *The War of the Rebellion: A Compilation of the Official Records of the Union and Confederate Armies* (Washington, D.C., 1880-1901), vol. XV part I, 517. Hereinafter cited as *OR*.
12   Foote, *The Civil War*, 549-56.
13   Ibid., 577-81.
14   Hartje, *Van Dorn*, 207-208.
15   *OR* vol. XVI, part I, 97-100.
16   Cozzins, *Iuka and Corinth*, 35.
17   Foote, *The Civil War*, 545; Ulysses S. Grant, *Memoirs and Selected Letters: Personal Memoirs of U.S. Grant, Selected Letters 1839-1865*, Mary Drake McFeely and William S. McFeely, eds., (New York: The Library of America, 1990), 264.
18   William S. Rosecrans, "The Battle of Corinth," *Battles and Leaders of the Civil War*, Robert Underwood Johnson and Clarence Clough Buel, eds. (New York: Castle Books, 1956), 740-41.
19   Lamers, *The Edge of Glory*, 91; Ephraim Anderson, *Memoirs: Historical and Personal; Including the Campaigns of the First Missouri Confederate Brigade*, 2nd ed. rev. (Dayton. Oh.: Morningside Bookshop, 1972), 219; *OR* vol. XVII, part I, 17, 175.
20   Grady McWhiney, *Braxton Bragg and Confederate Defeat*, Volume I: Field Command (New York: Columbia University Press, 1969), 267-71.
21   Ibid., 272-92.
22   Foote, *The Civil War*, 575-77; *OR* vol. XVII, part I, 749.
23   Anderson, *Memoirs: Historical and Personal*, 204.
24   Snead, "With Price," 727; *OR* vol. XVII, part I, 675.
25   *OR* vol. XVII, part I, 662, 665.
26   *OR* vol. XVII, part I, 682, 688; Cozzins, *Iuka and Corinth*, 46-49.

27 Foote, *The Civil War*, 585-669.
28 Foote, *The Civil War*, 665-66; *OR* vol. XVII, part I, 687.
29 Grant, *Memoirs*, 271; *OR* vol. XVII, part I, 133, 139, 210.
30 Cozzins, *Iuka and Corinth*, 50-57.
31 S.B. Barron, *The Lone Star Defenders: A Chronicle of the Third Texas Cavalry, Ross' Brigade* (New York: The Neale Publishing Co., 1908), 105.
32 R.S. Bevier, *History of the First and Second Missouri Confederate Brigades: 1861-1865 and From Wakarusa to Appomattox, A Military Anagraph* (St. Louis, Mo.: Bryan, Brand, & Company, 1879), 332; Sgt. Edwin H. Fay, *This Infernal War: The Confederate Letters of Edwin H. Fay*, Bell Irvin Wiley, ed. (Austin, Tex.: University of Texas Press, 1958), 158; David Garrett, *The Civil War Letters of David Garrett: Detailing the Adventures of the 6th Texas Cavalry 1861-1865*, Max Lale and Hobart Key, Jr., eds. (Marshall, Tex.: Port Caddo Press), 57.
33 *OR* vol. XVII, part I, 222, 228.
34 Cozzins, *Iuka and Corinth*, 60-65.

3. "The hardest-fought fight which I have ever witnessed"

1 William M. Lamers, *The Edge of Glory: A Biography of General William S. Rosecrans, U.S.A.* (New York: Harcourt, Brace & World, Inc., 1961), 103-105; Peter Cozzens, *The Darkest Days of the War: The Battles of Iuka and Corinth* (Chapel Hill, N.C.: University of North Carolina Press, 1997), 64; *The War of the Rebellion: A Compilation of the Official Records of the Union and Confederate Armies* (Washington, D.C., 1880-1901), vol. XVII part I, 224. Hereinafter cited as *OR*.
2 Cozzins, *Iuka and Corinth*, 68-70; "Thomas D. Christie to Alexander Christie, September 2nd, 1862," *Civil War Letters of the Christie Family* (Minnesota Historical Society) available from www.mnhs.org/library/Christie/td_christie.html (accessed March 11, 2005).
3 Cozzins, *Iuka and Corinth*, 68-70; *OR*, vol. XVII, part II, 66-67.
4 *OR*, vol. XVII, part II, 229-30.
5 Ibid., 229-30.
6 *OR*, vol. XVII, part I, 665, 697, 700.
7 Edwin C. Bearss, *Decision in Mississippi: Mississippi's Important Role in the War Between the States* (Jackson: Mississippi Commission on the War Between the States, 1962), 40-41.
8 *OR*, vol. XVII, part I, 69; Lamers, *Edge of Glory*, 108-109.
9 Lamers, *Edge of Glory*, 110; Cozzins, *Iuka and Corinth*, 73.
10 Bearss, *Decision in Mississippi*, 32-37; Alonzo L. Brown, *History of the Fourth Regiment of Minnesota Volunteers During the Great Rebellion 1861-1865* (St. Paul, Minn.: Pioneer Press Co., 1892), 81.
11 Bearss, *Decision in Mississippi*, 40-42; Cozzins, *Iuka and Corinth*, 78-80; Ephraim Anderson, *Memoirs: Historical and Personal: Including the Campaigns of the First Missouri Confederate Brigade*, 2nd ed. rev. (Dayton, Oh.: Morningside Bookshop, 1972), 222.
12 Victor M. Rose, *Ross's Texas Brigade* (Louisville, Ky.: Courier-Journal Book and Job Rooms, 1881), 72; Bearss, *Decision in Mississippi*, 42.
13 W.A.C., "Reminiscent Paragraphs," *Confederate Veteran*, IX (September 1893), 267; S.B. Barron, *The Lone Star Defenders: A Chronicle of the Third Texas Cavalry, Ross' Brigade* (New York: The Neale Publishing Co., 1908), 101-02; Cozzins, *Iuka and Corinth*, 86-87.
14 Cozzins, *Iuka and Corinth*, 82-83; Bearss, *Decision in Mississippi*, 38-39.
15 Lamers, *Edge of Glory*, 109-11; *OR*, vol. XVII, part I, 69.
16 Bearss, *Decision in Mississippi*, 39-40.
17 Cozzens, *Iuka and Corinth*, 80-87; Charles S. Hamilton, "The Battle of Iuka," *Battles and Leaders of the Civil War: North to Antietam*, Robert Underwood Johnson and Clarence Clough Buel, eds. (New York: Castle Books, 1956), 734-36.
18 Albert Castel, *General Sterling Price and the Civil War in the West* (Baton Rouge, La.: Louisiana State University Press, 1968), 87-88; G.W. Dudley, *The Battle of Iuka* (1896), 13; Cozzens, *Iuka and Corinth*, 86-87.
19 Bearss, *Decision in Mississippi*, 43; Rose, *Ross's Texas Brigade*, 70;
20 Lamers, *Edge of Glory*, 111.
21 W.P. Helm, "Close Fighting at Iuka, Mississippi" *Confederate Veteran*, XIX (April 1911), 171.

22   Cozzens, *Iuka and Corinth*, 90-91; Bearss, *Decision in Mississippi*, 44-45.
23   Bearss, *Decision in Mississippi*, 45-46; Helm, "Close Fighting at Iuka," 171.
24   Henry M. Neil, *A Battery at Close Quarters: A Paper read before the Ohio Commandery of the Loyal Legion* (Columbus, Oh.: The Champlin Press, 1909), 6-9.
25   Helm, "Close Fighting at Iuka," 171; Lamers, *Edge of Glory,* 111; Neil, *Paper at Loyal Legion,* 12.
26   Cozzens, *Iuka and Corinth*, 100-103; Dudley, *The Battle of Iuka* (1896), 7; Bearss, *Decision in Mississippi*, 52-53.
27   Bearss, *Decision in Mississippi*, 49-50; *OR*, vol. XVII, part II, 110.
28   Cozzins, *Iuka and Corinth*, 106-108; Mamie Yeary, *Reminiscences of the Boys in Gray: 1861-1865* (1912; rpt. ed., Dayton, Oh.: Morningside House, Inc., 1986), 1.
29   *OR*, vol. XVII, part I, 73, 88.
30   *OR*, vol. XVII, part I, 67, 122-23; Hamilton, "Battle of Iuka," 735.

4. "O, that Corinth could be left to take care of itself!"

1   Peter Cozzens, *The Darkest Days of the War: The Battles of Iuka and Corinth* (Chapel Hill, N.C.: University of North Carolina Press, 1997), 125-29; William M. Lamers, *The Edge of Glory: A Biography of General William S. Rosecrans, U.S.A.* (New York: Harcourt, Brace & World, Inc., 1961), 115; *The War of the Rebellion: A Compilation of the Official Records of the Union and Confederate Armies.* (Washington, D.C., 1880-1901), vol. XVII, part I, 67. Hereinafter cited as *OR*.
2   Edwin C. Bearss, *Decision in Mississippi: Mississippi's Important Role in the War Between the States* (Jackson: Mississippi Commission on the War Between the States, 1962), 54; R.S. Bevier, *History of the First and Second Missouri Confederate Brigades: 1861-1865 and From Wakarusa to Appomattox, A Military Anagraph* (St. Louis, Mo.: Bryan, Brand, & Company, 1879), 334; Ephraim Anderson, *Memoirs: Historical and Personal; Including the Campaigns of the First Missouri Confederate Brigade,* 2nd ed. rev. (Dayton, Oh.: Morningside Bookshop, 1972), 225.
3   Anderson, *Memoirs,* 223.
4   Ibid., 223-24.
5   Yeary, *Reminiscences,* 1. Surgeon A.C. Campbell, "Extracts from a Second Report of the Casualties at the Battle of Iuka, September 19, 1862," *The Medical and Surgical History of the Civil War,* 15 vols. (Wilmington, N.C.: Broadfoot Publishing Co., 1990), 2:248-49; Albert Castel, *General Sterling Price and the Civil War in the West* (Baton Rouge, La.: Louisiana State University Press, 1968), 103-104.
6   Frank Von Phul, "General Little's Burial: One of the Few Midnight Funerals in War or Peace," *Southern Historical Society Papers* (1901), 49 vols. rpt. ed. (Millwood, N.Y.: Kraus Reprint Co., 1978), 29:212-15; G.W. Dudley, *The Battle of Iuka* (1896), 15.
7   Von Phul, "General Little's Burial," 214-25.
8   Thomas L. Snead, "With Price East of the Mississippi," *Battles and Leaders of the Civil War: North to Antietam,* Robert Underwood Johnson and Clarence Clough Buel, eds. (New York: Castle Books, 1956), 733; Dabney Maury, "Recollections of Campaign against Grant in North Mississippi in 1862-63," *Southern Historical Society Papers* (1901), 49 vols. (rpt. ed; Millwood, N.Y.: Kraus Reprint Co., 1978), 13:289-90.
9   Maury, "Campaign against Grant," 290.
10   Snead, "With Price East of the Mississippi," 733; Cozzens, *Iuka and Corinth,* 120, 122-23; W.H. Tunnard, *A Southern Record: The History of the Third Regiment Louisiana Infantry,* 1866, rpt. ed. Edwin C. Bearss, ed. (Dayton, Oh.: Morningside Bookshop, 1970), 187-88.
11   Lamers, *The Edge of Glory,* 113-15; *OR*, vol. XVI part I, 74; Cozzins, *Iuka and Corinth,* 121-24.
12   Cozzins, *Iuka and Corinth* 129-30; Lamers, *Edge of Glory,* 117-19; Dr. Charles Ross, "Ssh! Battle in Progress!" *Civil War Times Illustrated,* XXXV (December 1996), 56-62.
13   Lamers, *Edge of Glory,* 127-28; Cozzins, *Iuka and Corinth,* 130; Oscar L. Jackson, *The Colonel's Diary,* David Prentice, ed. (Sharon, Penn.: 1922), 64.
14   *OR*, vol. XVII, part II, 68; Charles S. Hamilton, "The Battle of Iuka," *Battles and Leaders of the Civil War: North to Antietam,* Robert Underwood Johnson and Clarence Clough Buel, eds. (New York: Castle Books, 1956) 736; Cozzins, *Iuka and Corinth* 130-32.

[15] Alonzo L. Brown, *History of the Fourth Regiment of Minnesota Volunteers During the Great Rebellion 1861-1865* (St. Paul, Minn.: Pioneer Press Co., 1892), 96-97; Cyrus F. Boyd, *The Civil War Diary of Cyrus F. Boyd: Fifteenth Iowa Infantry 1861-1863*, Mildred Throne, ed. (Millwood, N.Y.: Kraus Reprint Co., 1977), 69.

[16] *OR*, vol. XVII, part II, 78, 123, 127, 133; Cozzins, *Iuka and Corinth*, 95, 133; Campbell, "Extracts," 248.

[17] Cozzins, *Iuka and Corinth*, 133-34; Bearss, *Decision in Mississippi*, 61-62.

[18] Boyd, *Civil War Diary*, 70 (punctuation added).

[19] S.B. Barron, *The Lone Star Defenders: A Chronicle of the Third Texas Cavalry, Ross' Brigade* (New York: The Neale Publishing Co., 1908), 109; Bearss, *Decision in Mississippi*, 60-62; Shelby Foote, *The Civil War: A Narrative, Fort Sumter to Perryville* (New York: Random House, Inc., 1958), 720-21.

[20] Cozzins, *Iuka and Corinth*, 143-48; *OR*, vol. XVII, part II, 234, 239; Lamers, *Edge of Glory*, 174-76.

[21] *OR*, vol. XVII, part I, 250; D. Leib Ambrose, *History of the Seventh Regiment Illinois Volunteer Infantry, from its first muster into the U.S. Service, April 25, 1862 to its final muster out, July 9, 1865* (Springfield, Ill.: Illinois Journal Company, 1868), 88-89.

5. "We shall sleep in Corinth to-night"

[1] *The War of the Rebellion: A Compilation of the Official Records of the Union and Confederate Armies.* (Washington, D.C., 1880-1901), vol. XVI part II, 665, 706. Hereinafter cited as *OR*.

[2] *OR*, vol. XVI part II, 718; William C. Davis, *The Orphan Brigade: The Kentucky Confederates Who Couldn't Go Home* (Garden City, N.Y.: Doubleday & Company, Inc., 1980), 111-24; Peter Cozzens, *The Darkest Days of the War: The Battles of Iuka and Corinth* (Chapel Hill, N.C.: University of North Carolina Press, 1997), 135-39; Shelby Foote, *The Civil War: A Narrative, Fort Sumter to Perryville* (New York: Random House, Inc., 1958), 720-22.

[3] *OR*, vol. XVII, part I, 377, part II, 691, 712.

[4] Ibid., 713; Grady McWhiney, *Braxton Bragg and Confederate Defeat* Volume I: Field Command (New York: Columbia University Press, 1969), 295.

[5] Robert G. Hartje, *Van Dorn: The Life and Times of a Confederate General*, (Nashville, Tenn.: Vanderbilt University Press, 1967), 214-16; Arthur B. Carter, *The Tarnished Cavalier: Major General Earl Van Dorn, CSA* (Knoxville, Tenn.: University of Tennessee Press, 1999), 90-92; *OR*, vol. XVII, part I, 377, 452.

[6] *OR*, vol. XVII, part I, 377.

[7] Hartje, *Van Dorn*, 214-15; Albert Castel, *General Sterling Price and the Civil War in the West* (Baton Rouge, La.: Louisiana State University Press, 1968), 108-109; *OR*, vol. XVII, part I, 377, 453.

[8] Castel, *General Sterling Price*, 106-107; Cozzins, *Iuka and Corinth*, 139-40; *OR*, vol. XVII, part I, 441, 453.

[9] *OR*, vol. LII, part I, 365-69; Robert G. Hartje, "Major General Earl Van Dorn" (Unpublished doctoral dissertation, Vanderbilt University, Nashville, 1955), 296.

[10] *OR*, vol. XVII, part II, 715; Carter, *Tarnished Cavalier*, 91.

[11] Cozzins, *Iuka and Corinth*, 136-37; Carter, *Tarnished Cavalier*, 90-92; Hartje, *Van Dorn*, 214-16; Foote, *The Civil War*, 720-22; William M. Lamers, *The Edge of Glory: A Biography of General William S. Rosecrans, U.S.A.* (New York: Harcourt, Brace & World, Inc., 1961), 94-95, 133.

[12] *OR*, vol. XVII, part I, 417; W.H. Tunnard, *A Southern Record: The History of the Third Regiment Louisiana Infantry*, 1866, rpt. ed. Edwin C. Bearss, ed. (Dayton, Oh.: Morningside Bookshop, 1970), 191.

[13] *OR*, vol. XVII, part II, 71, 246; Cozzins, *Iuka and Corinth*, 145-46; Lamers, *Edge of Glory*, 133-34; Foote, *The Civil War*, 722.

[14] William S. Rosecrans, "The Battle of Corinth," *Battles and Leaders of the Civil War: North to Antietam*, Robert Underwood Johnson and Clarence Clough Buel, eds. (New York: Castle Books, 1956), 743; Cozzins, *Iuka and Corinth*, 152-53; Lamers, *Edge of Glory*, 135-36.

[15] Cozzins, *Iuka and Corinth*, 155-60; Carter, *Tarnished Cavalier*, 95-96; Hartje, *Van Dorn*, 221-23; Castel, *General Sterling Price*, 110; Ephraim Anderson, *Memoirs: Historical and Personal; Including the Campaigns of the First Missouri Confederate Brigade*, 2nd ed. rev. (Dayton, Oh.: Morningside Bookshop, 1972), 231.

16   Cozzins, *Iuka and Corinth*, 157, 166; Rosecrans, "Battle of Corinth, 746; *OR*, vol. XVII, part I, 408.

17   Cozzins, *Iuka and Corinth*, 166-74; William Barnaby Faherty, *Exile in Erin: A Confederate Chaplain's Story, the Life of Father John B. Bannon* (St. Louis, Mo.: Missouri Historical Society Press, 2002), 47; Carter, *Tarnished Cavalier*, 96-97; Dr. W.C. Holmes, "The Battle of Corinth," *Confederate Veteran*, XXVII, (August 1919), 291; Frank Carter, "The Capture of the Lady Richardson," *Confederate Veteran*, III, (October 1895), 306.

18   Cozzins, *Iuka and Corinth*, 175-81; Castel, *General Sterling Price*, 110-11; R.S. Bevier, *History of the First and Second Missouri Confederate Brigades: 1861-1865 and From Wakarusa to Appomattox, A Military Anagraph* (St. Louis, Mo.: Bryan, Brand, & Company, 1879), 337.

19   D. Leib Ambrose, *History of the Seventh Regiment Illinois Volunteer Infantry, from its first muster into the U.S. Service, April 25, 1862 to its final muster out, July 9, 1865* (Springfield, Ill.: Illinois Journal Company, 1868), 95; Cyrus F. Boyd, *The Civil War Diary of Cyrus F. Boyd: Fifteenth Iowa Infantry 1861-1863*, Mildred Throne, ed. (Millwood, N.Y.: Kraus Reprint Co., 1977), 72; Cozzins, *Iuka and Corinth*, 181-93.

20   Cozzins, *Iuka and Corinth*, 194-207; Castel, *General Sterling Price*, 111; *OR*, vol. XVII, part I, 255.

21   Cozzins, *Iuka and Corinth*, 206; James E. Payne, "The Sixth Missouri at Corinth." *Confederate Veteran*, XXXVI, (December 1928), 464; *OR*, vol. XVII, part I, 277.

22   Newton A. Keen, *Living and Fighting with the Texas 6th Cavalry* (Gaithersburg, Md.: Butternut Press, Inc., 1988), 38-39; Cloyd Bryner, *Bugle Echoes: The Story of Illinois 47th* (Springfield, Ill.: Philips Bros. Printers and Binders, 1905), 59-60; Cozzins, *Iuka and Corinth*, 209-13.

23   Cozzins, *Iuka and Corinth*, 200-202, 216-20; Lamers, *Edge of Glory*, 140-41; Rosecrans, "Battle of Corinth, 746-47.

24   Cozzins, *Iuka and Corinth*, 214-16; Hartje, *Van Dorn*, 225-26; Castel, *General Sterling Price*, 113; *OR*, vol. XVII, part I, 379.

6. "War to the knife"

1   Peter Cozzens, *The Darkest Days of the War: The Battles of Iuka and Corinth* (Chapel Hill, N.C.: University of North Carolina Press, 1997), 224-28; William M. Lamers, *The Edge of Glory: A Biography of General William S. Rosecrans, U.S.A.* (New York: Harcourt, Brace & World, Inc., 1961), 142-43; *The War of the Rebellion: A Compilation of the Official Records of the Union and Confederate Armies* (Washington, D.C., 1880-1901), vol. XVI part I, 257-58. Hereinafter cited as *OR*.

2   *OR*, vol. XVII, part I, 161; Cozzins, *Iuka and Corinth*, 227-28; Lamers, *Edge of Glory*, 134-45; William S. Rosecrans, "The Battle of Corinth," *Battles and Leaders of the Civil War: North to Antietam*, Robert Underwood Johnson and Clarence Clough Buel, eds. (New York: Castle Books, 1956), 748; Stacy D. Allen, "Corinth, Mississippi: Crossroads of the Western Confederacy," *Blue & Gray Magazine*, XIX (August 2002), 44.

3   Rosecrans, "Battle of Corinth," 748-49; Cozzins, *Iuka and Corinth*, 228-33; Lamers, *Edge of Glory*, 145-46; Robert G. Hartje, *Van Dorn: The Life and Times of a Confederate General* (Nashville, Tenn.: Vanderbilt University Press, 1967), 228-29; *OR*, vol. XVII, part I, 431.

4   Allen, "Corinth, Crossroads," 38-42; Cozzins, *Iuka and Corinth*, 228-30; R.S. Bevier, *History of the First and Second Missouri Confederate Brigades: 1861-1865 and From Wakarusa to Appomattox, A Military Anagraph* (St. Louis, Mo.: Bryan, Brand, & Company, 1879), 338.

5   Cozzins, *Iuka and Corinth*, 232-35; Lamers, *Edge of Glory*, 146-47; Hartje, *Van Dorn*, 229.

6   Cozzins, *Iuka and Corinth*, 235-36; Hartje, *Van Dorn*, 229; Robert Collins Suhr, "Attack Written Deep and Crimson," *TheHistoryNet.com*, available from www.historynet.com/acw/blattack/index.html (accessed February 16, 2005).

7   Cozzins, *Iuka and Corinth*, 237; Allen, "Corinth, Crossroads," 42; Shelby Foote, *The Civil War: A Narrative, Fort Sumter to Perryville* (New York: Random House, Inc., 1958), 723-24.

8   Cozzins, *Iuka and Corinth*, 240-41; Lamers, *Edge of Glory*, 133; Rosecrans, "Battle of Corinth," 741; James E. Payne, "The Sixth Missouri at Corinth," *Confederate Veteran*, XXXVI, (December 1928), 464; Ephraim Anderson, *Memoirs: Historical and Personal; Including the Campaigns of the First Missouri Confederate Brigade*, 2nd ed. rev. (Dayton, Oh.: Morningside Bookshop, 1972), 237.

9   Cozzins, *Iuka and Corinth*, 241-42; Payne, "Sixth Missouri," 464; *OR*, vol. XVII, part I, 259.

10   Cozzins, *Iuka and Corinth*, 242-45; Payne, "Sixth Missouri," 464.

11   Cozzins, *Iuka and Corinth*, 227, 250-51; Henry M. Neil, *A Battery at Close Quarters: A Paper read before the Ohio Commandery of the Loyal Legion* (Columbus, Oh.: The Champlin Press, 1909) 15, 19, 28.

12   Cozzins, *Iuka and Corinth*, 245-51; Bevier, *History*, 341; *OR*, vol. XVII, part I, 401; Payne, "Sixth Missouri," 464.

13   Cozzins, *Iuka and Corinth*, 253-56; Allen, "Corinth, Crossroads," 42-43; Foote, *The Civil War*, 724; Rosecrans, "Battle of Corinth," 749; J.A. McKinstry, "With Col. Rogers When He Fell," *Confederate Veteran*, IV, (July 1896), 220-21.

14   Joseph E. Chance, *The Second Texas Infantry: From Shiloh to Vicksburg* (Austin, Tex.: Eakin Press, 1984), 1-40, 70-73; Cozzins, *Iuka and Corinth*, 253-55.

15   Oscar L. Jackson, *The Colonel's Diary*, David Prentice, ed. (Sharon, Penn.: 1922), 71; Cozzins, *Iuka and Corinth*, 255-58.

16   Jackson, *The Colonel's Diary*, 72, 86.

17   Jackson, *The Colonel's Diary*, 73, 86; Cozzins, *Iuka and Corinth*, 259-61.

18   Jackson, *The Colonel's Diary*, 73-74, 86; Cozzins, *Iuka and Corinth*, 261-63; Allen, "Corinth, Crossroads," 38, 42-43.

19   McKinstry, "With Col. Rogers," 221; Jackson, *The Colonel's Diary*, 86-87; Cozzins, *Iuka and Corinth*, 263-65; Allen, "Corinth, Crossroads," 43; Cloyd Bryner, *Bugle Echoes: The Story of Illinois 47th* (Springfield, Ill.: Philips Bros. Printers and Binders, 1905), 59-60; Cyrus F. Boyd, *The Civil War Diary of Cyrus F. Boyd: Fifteenth Iowa Infantry 1861-1863*, Mildred Throne, ed. (Millwood, N.Y.: Kraus Reprint Co., 1977), 75.

20   Jackson, *The Colonel's Diary*, 87; Cozzins, *Iuka and Corinth*, 265-66; Chance, *Second Texas*, 75-76; Newton A. Keen, *Living and Fighting with the Texas 6th Cavalry* (Gaithersburg, Md.: Butternut Press, Inc., 1986), 40-41.

21   Boyd, *Civil War Diary*, 75; *OR*, vol. XVII, part I, 169-70; Rosecrans, "Battle of Corinth," 749.

22   Cozzins, *Iuka and Corinth*, 267-69; Rosecrans, "Battle of Corinth," 750, 753; Allen, "Corinth, Crossroads," 43-44; Lamers, *Edge of Glory*, 148-52; Bryner, *Bugle Echoes*, 174; Ras Stirman. *In Fine Spirits: The Civil War Letters of Ras Stirman, With Historical Comments by Pat Carr* (Fayetteville, Ark.: Washington County Historical Society, 1986), 52.

23   Cozzins, *Iuka and Corinth*, 271-72; Hartje, *Van Dorn*, 232-33; Arthur B. Carter, *The Tarnished Cavalier: Major General Earl Van Dorn, CSA* (Knoxville, Tenn.: University of Tennessee Press, 1999), 103-104; *OR*, vol. XVII, part I, 422.

24   Albert Castel, *General Sterling Price and the Civil War in the West* (Baton Rouge, La.: Louisiana State University Press, 1968), 118; Dabney Maury, "Recollections of Campaign Against Grant in North Mississippi in 1862-63," *Southern Historical Society Papers* 1901, 49 vols. rpt. ed. (Millwood, N.Y.: Kraus Reprint Co., 1978), 8:299.

25   Dabney Maury, "Recollections of General Earl Van Dorn," *Southern Historical Society Papers* 1901, 49 vols. rpt. ed. (Millwood, N.Y.: Kraus Reprint Co., 1978), 19:195; Maury, "Campaign against Grant," 8:299; Cozzins, *Iuka and Corinth*, 270-73, 276-79; Carter, *Tarnished Cavalier*, 104.

7. "Git out o' thar tail-end first"

1   Peter Cozzens, *The Darkest Days of the War: The Battles of Iuka and Corinth* (Chapel Hill, N.C.: University of North Carolina Press, 1997), 273-74; Cyrus F. Boyd, *The Civil War Diary of Cyrus F. Boyd: Fifteenth Iowa Infantry 1861-1863*, Mildred Throne, ed. (Millwood, N.Y.: Kraus Reprint Co., 1977), 76; Dabney Maury, *Recollections of a Virginian in the Mexican, Indian, and Civil Wars* (New York: Charles Scribner's Sons, 1894), 171; William M. Lamers, *The Edge of Glory: A Biography of General William S. Rosecrans, U.S.A.* (New York: Harcourt, Brace & World, Inc., 1961), 154.

2   Cozzens, *Iuka and Corinth*, 275-77; Lamers, *Edge of Glory*, 155-58.

3   Dabney Maury, "Recollections of Campaign Against Grant in North Mississippi in 1862-63," *Southern Historical Society Papers* 1901, 49 vols. rpt. ed. (Millwood, N.Y.: Kraus Reprint Co., 1978), 8:302; Robert G. Hartje, *Van Dorn; The Life and Times of a Confederate General*, (Nashville, Tenn.: Vanderbilt University Press, 1967), 234; Arthur B. Carter, *The Tarnished Cavalier: Major General Earl Van Dorn, CSA* (Knoxville, Tenn.: University of Tennessee Press, 1999), 104-105; Cozzins, *Iuka and Corinth*, 277-78.

4   Albert Castel, *General Sterling Price and the Civil War in the West* (Baton Rouge, La.: Louisiana State University Press, 1968), 119-20; Dabney Maury, "Recollections of General Earl Van Dorn," *Southern Historical Society Papers* 1901, 49 vols. rpt. ed. (Millwood, N.Y.: Kraus Reprint Co., 1978), 19:196; Carter, *The Tarnished Cavalier*, 104-105; Cozzins, *Iuka and Corinth*, 278.

5   *The War of the Rebellion: A Compilation of the Official Records of the Union and Confederate Armies*. (Washington, D.C., 1880-1901), vol. XVI part I, 155. Hereinafter cited as *OR*; Cozzins, *Iuka and Corinth*, 293-94; Lamers, *Edge of Glory*, 160-62.

6   Boyd, *Civil War Diary*, 76; Cozzins, *Iuka and Corinth*, 294-96; Lamers, *Edge of Glory*, 162-63.

7   Maury, "Campaign Against Grant," 303; Stacy D. Allen, "Corinth, Mississippi: Crossroads of the Western Confederacy," *Blue & Gray Magazine*, XIX (August 2002), 45; Cozzins, *Iuka and Corinth*, 294-96.

8   Ephraim Anderson, *Memoirs: Historical and Personal; Including the Campaigns of the First Missouri Confederate Brigade*, 2nd ed. rev. (Dayton, Oh.: Morningside Bookshop, 1972), 241.

9   Cozzins, *Iuka and Corinth*, 280-92; Allen, "Corinth, Crossroads," 45; *Ras Stirman, In Fine Spirits: The Civil War Letters of Ras Stirman, with Historical Comments by Pat Carr* (Fayetteville, Ark.: Washington County Historical Society, 1986), 53.

10 Cozzins, *Iuka and Corinth*, 291-97; Castel, *General Sterling Price*, 121-22; Hartje, *Van Dorn*, 236-38; R.S. Bevier, *History of the First and Second Missouri Confederate Brigades: 1861-1865 and From Wakarusa to Appomattox, A Military Anagraph* (St. Louis, Mo.: Bryan, Brand, & Company, 1879), 344.

11 Cozzins, *Iuka and Corinth*, 298-302; Lamers, *Edge of Glory*, 167-68; *OR*, vol. XVII, part I, 156, 163.

12 Cozzins, *Iuka and Corinth*, 302-304; Lamers, *Edge of Glory*, 168-80; William S. Rosecrans, "The Battle of Corinth," *Battles and Leaders of the Civil War: North to Antietam*, Robert Underwood Johnson and Clarence Clough Buel, eds. (New York: Castle Books, 1956), 755; Maury, "Campaign Against Grant," 305.

13 Cozzins, *Iuka and Corinth*, 300-305; *OR*, vol. XVII, part I, 400; Dr. W.C. Holmes, "The Battle of Corinth," *Confederate Veteran*, XXVII, (August 1919), 292; Edwin H. Fay, *This Infernal War: The Confederate Letters of Sgt. Edwin H Fay*, Bell Irvin Wiley, ed. (Austin, Tex.: University of Texas Press, 1958), 165.

14 *OR*, vol. XVII, part I, 176, 304, 382-84, 397; Edward H. Bonekemper III, *A Victor, Not A Butcher: Ulysses S. Grant's Overlooked Military Genius* (Washington, D.C.: Regnery Publishing, Inc., 2004), 292-94; Cozzins, *Iuka and Corinth*, 305-306; Allen, "Corinth, Crossroads," 45-46; *Handbook of Texas Online*, s.v. "ROGERS, WILLIAM PELEG," www.tsha.utexas.edu/handbook/online/articles/RR/fro64.html (accessed August 16, 2005).

15 Cozzins, *Iuka and Corinth*, 317-18; Quoted in Grady McWhiney, *Braxton Bragg and Confederate Defeat* Volume I: Field Command (New York: Columbia University Press, 1969), 321.

16 Cozzins, *Iuka and Corinth*, 315-19; William T. Sherman, *Memoirs of General W.T. Sherman*, Charles Royster, ed. (New York: The Library of America, 1990), 284; Fay, *This Infernal War*, 165.

17 Cozzins, *Iuka and Corinth*, 306-10, 322-23; Hartje, *Van Dorn*, 239-45, Quoted in Carter, *The Tarnished Cavalier*, 107-115, 119.

18 Cozzins, *Iuka and Corinth*, 322-23; Quoted in John Allan Wyeth, *That Devil Forrest: Life of General Nathan Bedford Forrest* (New York: Harper & Brothers, Publishers, 1959), 156-57.

19 Cozzins, *Iuka and Corinth*, 323-24; Robert G. Hartje, "Major General Earl Van Dorn" (Unpublished doctoral dissertation, Vanderbilt University, Nashville, 1955), 285.

20   Victor M. Rose, *Ross's Texas Brigade* (Louisville, Ky.: Courier-Journal Book and Job Rooms, 1881), 99; George L. Griscom, *Fighting With Ross' Texas Cavalry Brigade, C.S.A.: Diary of Lieut. George L. Griscom, Adjutant, 9th Texas Cavalry Regiment,* Homer L. Kerr, ed. (Hillsboro, Tex.: Hill Junior College Press, 1976), 65; Judith Lee Hallock, ed., *The Civil War Letters of Joshua K. Calloway* (Athens: University of Georgia Press, 1997), 88; Newton A. Keen, *Living and Fighting with the Texas 6th Cavalry* (Gaithersburg, Md.: Butternut Press, Inc., 1986), 47.

21   Cozzins, *Iuka and Corinth,* 321-22; Castel, General Sterling Price, 125-27.

22   Cozzins, *Iuka and Corinth,* 310-14; Lamers, *Edge of Glory,* 170-80; Ulysses S. Grant, *Memoirs and Selected Letters: Personal Memoirs of U.S. Grant, Selected Letters 1839-1865,* Mary Drake McFeely and William S. McFeely, eds. (New York: The Library of America, 1990), 281-82.

23   Grant, *Memoirs,* 281.

Appendix A

Order of Battle
Battle of Iuka
September 19, 1862

CONFEDERATE ARMY OF THE WEST
MAJ. GEN. STERLING PRICE, COMMANDING

FIRST DIVISON: Brig. General Henry Little (k), Brig. Gen. Louis Hébert

COL. ELIJAH GATES'S BRIGADE
16th Arkansas
2d Missouri
3d Missouri
1st Missouri Dismounted Cavalry

BRIG. GEN. LOUIS HÉBERT'S BRIGADE
14th Arkansas
17th Arkansas
3d Louisiana
40th Mississippi
1st Texas Legion
3d Texas Dismounted Cavalry

BRIG. GEN. MARTIN E. GREEN'S BRIGADE
7th Mississippi Battalion
43rd Mississippi
4th Missouri
6th Missouri
3d Missouri Dismounted Cavalry

COL. JOHN D. MARTIN'S BRIGADE
37th Alabama
36th Mississippi
37th Mississippi
38th Mississippi

ARTILLERY
Clark Missouri Battery
Dawson's St. Louis Battery
Guibor's Missouri Battery
Landis's Missouri Battery
Wade's Missouri Battery

CAVALRY
Brig. Gen. Frank C. Armstrong
Adam's Mississippi Regiment
2d Arkansas
2d Missouri
4th Mississippi Cavalry
1st Mississippi Partisan Rangers

UNION ARMY OF THE MISSISSIPPI
MAJ. GEN. WILLIAM S. ROSECRANS, COMMANDING

SECOND DIVISION: Brig. David S. Stanley

COL. JOHN W. FULLER'S BRIGADE
27th Ohio
39th Ohio
43rd Ohio
63rd Ohio

COL. JOSEPH A. MOWER'S BRIGADE
26th Illinois
47th Illinois
11th Missouri
8th Wisconsin

THIRD DIVISON: Brig. Gen. Charles S. Hamilton

COL. JOHN B. SANBORN'S BRIGADE
48th Indiana
5th Iowa
16th Iowa
4th Minnesota
26th Missouri

BRIG. GEN. JEREMIAH C. SULLIVAN'S BRIGADE
10th Iowa
17th Iowa
10th Missouri
80th Ohio
Company F, 24th Missouri

ARTILLERY
2d Battery, Iowa Light Artillery
3d Battery, Michigan Light Artillery
Battery M, 1st Missouri Light Artillery
11th Battery, Ohio Light Artillery
Battery F, 2d U.S. Artillery
8th Battery, Wisconsin Light Artillery
12th Battery, Wisconsin Light Artillery

CAVALRY
COL. JOHN K. MIZNER
2d Iowa
3d Michigan
Companies B and E, 7th Kansas
Jenk's Company, Illinois Cavalry

APPENDIX B

Order of Battle
Battle of Corinth
October 3-4, 1862

ARMY OF THE WEST (Price's Corps)

MAJ. GEN. STERLING PRICE

FIRST DIVISON: Brig. Gen. Louis Hébert, Brig. Gen. Martin E. Green

COL. ELIJAH GATES'S BRIGADE
16th Arkansas
2d Missouri
3d Missouri
5th Missouri
1st Missouri Dismounted Cavalry

COL. W. BRUCE COLBERT'S BRIGADE
14th Arkansas
17th Arkansas
3d Louisiana
40th Mississippi
1st Texas Legion
3d Texas Dismounted Cavalry

BRIG. GEN. MARTIN E. GREEN'S BRIGADE
Brig. Gen. Martin E. Green, Col. W. H. Moore (mw)
7th Mississippi Battalion
43rd Mississippi
4th Missouri
6th Missouri
3d Missouri Dismounted Cavalry

COL. JOHN D. MARTIN'S BRIGADE
Col. John D. Martin (mw), Col. Robert McLain (w)
37th Alabama
36th Mississippi
37th Mississippi
38th Mississippi

ARTILLERY
Clark Missouri Battery
Dawson's St. Louis Battery
Guibor's Missouri Battery
Landis's Missouri Battery
Lucas's Battery
Wade's Missouri Battery

SECOND DIVISON: Brig. General Dabney H. Maury

BRIG. GEN. JOHN C. MOORE'S BRIGADE
42d Alabama
15th Arkansas
23rd Arkansas
35th Mississippi
2d Texas

BRIG. GEN. W. L. CABELL'S BRIGADE
18th Arkansas
19th Arkansas
20th Arkansas
21st Arkansas
Jones's Arkansas Battalion
Rapley's Arkansas Battalion

BRIG. GEN. C. W. PHIFER'S BRIGADE
3d Arkansas Dismounted Cavalry
6th Texas Dismounted Cavalry
9th Texas Dismounted Cavalry
Stirman's Arkansas Sharpshooters

ARTILLERY
Appeal Battery
Bledsoe's Missouri Battery
McNally's Battery

RESERVE ARTILLERY
Hoxton's Tennessee Battery
Sengstak's Battery

CAVALRY
Brig. Gen. Frank C. Armstrong
Slemon's Regiment
Wirt Adams's Mississippi Regiment

VAN DORN'S DISTRICT OF THE MISSISSIPPI

FIRST DIVISON: Maj. Gen. Mansfield Lovell

BRIG. GEN. ALBERT RUST'S BRIGADE
4th Alabama Battalion
31st Alabama
35th Alabama
9th Arkansas
3d Kentucky
7th Kentucky

BRIG. GEN. JOHN VILLEPIGUE'S BRIGADE
33d Mississippi
39th Mississippi

BRIG. GEN. JOHN BOWEN'S BRIGADE
6th Mississippi
15th Mississippi
22d Mississippi
Caruthers's Mississippi Battalion
1st Missouri

ARTILLERY
Hudson's Battery
Watson's Battery

CAVALRY
Col. W. H. Jackson
1st Mississippi
7th Tennessee

UNION ARMY OF THE MISSISSIPPI
Maj. Gen. William S. Rosecrans, Commanding

SECOND DIVISION: Brig. David S. Stanley

COL. JOHN W. FULLER'S BRIGADE
27th Ohio
39th Ohio
43rd Ohio
63rd Ohio

COL. JOSEPH A. MOWER'S BRIGADE
26th Illinois
47th Illinois
5th Minnesota
11th Missouri
8th Wisconsin

THIRD DIVISON: Brig. Gen. Charles S. Hamilton

BRIG. GEN. NAPOLEON BUFORD'S BRIGADE
48th Indiana
59th Indiana
5th Iowa
16th Iowa
4th Minnesota
26th Missouri

BRIG. GEN. JEREMIAH C. SULLIVAN'S BRIGADE
Brig. Gen. Jeremiah C. Sullivan (w), Col. Samuel A. Holmes
56th Illinois
10th Iowa
17th Iowa
10th Missouri
80th Ohio
Company F, 24th Missouri

ARTILLERY
2d Battery, Iowa Light Artillery
3d Battery, Michigan Light Artillery
Battery M, 1st Missouri Light Artillery
11th Battery, Ohio Light Artillery
Battery F, 2d U.S. Artillery
6th Battery, Wisconsin Light Artillery
8th Battery, Wisconsin Light Artillery
12th Battery, Wisconsin Light Artillery

CAVALRY
Col. John K. Mizner
2d Iowa
3d Michigan
Companies B and E, 7th Kansas
Jenk's Company, Illinois Cavalry

UNATTACHED
64th Illinois (Yates Sharpshooters)
Companies A, B, C, D, H, and I Siege Artillery
1st U.S. Infantry

FEDERAL ARMY OF WEST TENNESSEE

SECOND DIVISION: Brig. Gen. Thomas A. Davies

BRIG. GEN. PLEASANT A. HACKLEMAN'S BRIGADE
Brig. Gen. Pleasant A. Hackleman (mw), Col. Thomas Sweeny
52d Illinois
2d Iowa
7th Iowa
58th Illinois (detachment)
8th Iowa (detachment)
12th Iowa (detachment)
14th Iowa (detachment)

BRIG. GEN. RICHARD J. OGLESBY'S BRIGADE
Brig. Gen. Richard J. Oglesby (w), Col. August Mersy
9th Illinois
12th Illinois
22d Ohio
81st Ohio

COL. SILAS D. BALDWIN'S BRIGADE
Col. Silas D. Baldwin (w), Col. John V. Du Bois
7th Illinois
50th Illinois
57th Illinois

SIXTH DIVISION: Brig. Gen. Thomas J. McKean

COL. BENJAMIN ALLEN'S BRIGADE
Col. Benjamin Allen, Brig. Gen. John McArthur
21st Missouri
16th Wisconsin
17th Wisconsin

COL. JOHN OLIVER'S BRIGADE
Ford's Company, Illinois Cavalry
15th Michigan
Companies A, B, C, and E, 18th Missouri
14th Wisconsin
18th Wisconsin

COL. MARCELLUS M. CROCKER
11th Iowa
13th Iowa
15th Iowa
16th Iowa

UNATTACHED
14th Missouri (Western Sharpshooters)

ARTILLERY
Capt. Andrew Hickenlooper
Battery F, 2d Illinois Light Artillery
1st Battery, Minnesota Light Artillery
3d, 5th, and 10th Batteries, Ohio Light Artillery

APPENDIX C

Order of Battle
Battle of Davis Bridge
October 5, 1862

CONFEDERATE ARMY OF WEST TENNESSEE
MAJ. GEN. EARL VAN DORN, COMMANDING

SECOND DIVISON: Brig. General Dabney H. Maury

BRIG. GEN. JOHN C. MOORE'S BRIGADE
42d Alabama
15th Arkansas
23rd Arkansas
35th Mississippi
2d Texas

BRIG. GEN. W. L. CABELL'S BRIGADE
18th Arkansas
19th Arkansas
20th Arkansas
21st Arkansas
Jones's Arkansas Battalion
Rapley's Arkansas Battalion

BRIG. GEN. C. W. PHIFER'S BRIGADE
Col. Lawrence S. Ross
3d Arkansas Dismounted Cavalry
6th Texas Dismounted Cavalry
9th Texas Dismounted Cavalry
Stirman's Arkansas Sharpshooters

ARTILLERY
Appeal Battery
Bledsoe's Missouri Battery
Dawson's St. Louis Battery
McNally's Battery

CAVALRY
Wirt Adams's Mississippi Regiment

FEDERAL ARMY OF WEST TENNESSEE

FOURTH DIVISION: Maj. Gen. Stephen A. Hurlbut

Escort
Company A, 2d Illinois Cavalry

BRIG. GEN. JACOB G. LAUMAN'S BRIGADE
28th Illinois
32d Illinois
41st Illinois
53d Illinois
3d Iowa

BRIG. GEN. JAMES C. VEATCH'S BRIGADE
14th Illinois
15th Illinois
46th Illinois
25th Indiana
53d Indiana

PROVISIONAL BRIGADE
Col. Robert K. Scott
12th Michigan
68th Ohio

ARTILLERY
Battery L, 2d Illinois Light Artillery
1st Missouri Light Artillery
7th Battery, Ohio Light Artillery
15th Battery, Ohio Light Artillery

CAVALRY
1st and 2d Battalions, 5th Ohio Cavalry

INDEX